Blessed are the Poor?

Blessed Are the Poor?

Urban Poverty and the Church

Laurie Green

scm press

Published in 2015 by SCM Press
Editorial office
3rd Floor
Invicta House
108-114 Golden Lane,
London
EC1Y 0TG

SCM Press is an imprint of Hymns Ancient & Modern Ltd
(a registered charity)
13A Hellesdon Park Road
Norwich NR6 5DR, UK

www.scmpress.co.uk

British Library Cataloguing in Publication data

A catalogue record for this book is available from the British Library

978 0 334 05365 1

Typeset by Manila Typesetting
Printed and bound by
CPI Group (UK) Ltd, Croydon

Contents

Acknowledgements

I owe a great debt of gratitude to so many, especially all those who have been prepared to sit with me and tell me their challenging and inspiring stories. The Church Urban Fund has been generous in paying my train costs to travel from estate to estate across the country, and projects and churches have willingly opened their doors to me and shared their joys, successes, mistakes and wonderful hospitality. Without their help this book could never have been written. I'm also grateful to Natalie Watson and her SCM team, to Jane Winter, Peter Knight and Vicki for commenting on early drafts, and to Anthony Harvey for that lovely soup and coffee at the British Library along with his scholarly advice. David Ford and Rowan Williams have shared their thoughts, and Monodeep Daniel gave me an evening of fireside theology and wonderful curry at the Delhi Brotherhood. My beloved sisters at St Mary's Abbey at West Malling supported me by their example and their prayer, and the members and Executive of the National Estate Churches Network have been there throughout. But it was my wife Vicki to whom I once again broke my promise never to write another book and to whom I owe so very much in seeing me through with everlasting cups of tea! I hope they all feel this book was worth all their help and encouragement. Thanks to you and all the others.

+Laurie

Introduction:

The Crucial Question

What did Jesus really mean when he looked at his followers and announced, 'Blessed are you who are poor'? I have struggled for many years to understand just what he meant by that pronouncement and have never found any of the usual answers to be at all satisfying. Those of us who have been poor, or lived with poor people for substantial parts of our lives or ministries, are only too aware that the lives of the poor are blighted by lack of opportunity and exclusion. They live shorter lives and have distinctly poor prospects. How then can Jesus call such people blessed? It would appear that the Church through the centuries has found this particular teaching so profoundly unsettling that it has either assumed that Jesus did not mean what he said, that he was simply exaggerating for effect, or that he was putting a rather romantic gloss on the real situation that confronts the poor. But if Jesus did not quite mean what he said, why did he make a life for himself in their midst? Why would he people his stories with outcasts, spend time healing those who were poor and destitute, and even die alongside them on a cross? All this is anything but exaggeration for effect! It was from this deep commitment that Jesus went on to suggest that the rich, on the other hand, have a very slim chance of entering the Kingdom of God – it would be easier for a camel to thread its way through the eye of a needle. When his first disciples heard this teaching, they were as aghast as we are and found it very hard to believe. Yet despite all the obvious pressures that there must have been on the early Christians to omit these teachings from the Gospel records, there they still stand as a challenging testimony to the mind of a Jesus who clearly saw things very differently from how we prefer to see them.

I had an important decision to make in 1970. I had just completed my preparatory studies in readiness for ordination. Those studies had taken me from London across to New York and back to Canterbury, the originating diocese of the Church of England. Dean Sydney Evans had just interviewed me about where I might begin my ordained ministry and had sent me off with my new wife Vicki to visit a likely parish. So there we were, huddled in the back of a rather large saloon car being driven by the parish rector and surrounded by the other members of his parish staff. The rector was very keen to impress, and in many ways he had reason to be proud of his team's achievements. The parish church was extraordinarily large, and he proudly boasted that they nearly filled it with willing members every Sunday. He was now driving us around the rather prosperous neighbourhood and chanced to look across to the right where stood houses of a distinctly lower quality than those we had so far viewed. He saw me looking more intently at them and, hoping to quell my fears, remarked: 'Oh, that's our council housing estate. But don't worry, they don't ever bother us.' And on hearing that, my decision was made. I wanted to spend the rest of my ministry living in those areas that others like to ignore.

Vicki and I returned to Dean Evans to explain our concern, and immediately he wisely sent us to visit a very different sort of parish in Birmingham – at that time still the heavily industrialized 'second city' of England. Just before World War Two Birmingham City Council had begun building what turned out to be at that time the largest expanse of publicly built housing in the whole of Europe. And right at the heart of that enormous housing estate was the Parish of St Mark, Kingstanding, which was to become our home for the next four years. We've never looked back.

Some 30 years later a newly ordained young man said to me:

> When I first arrived in the housing estate where I was to minister, I was terrified. I had heard so many stories about the brutality and ugliness of the neighbourhood. I felt as if my hands

> had been tied behind my back, and I was being thrown into the fiery furnace. But after being here three years I've come to realize that the estate and its people have burnt away those fetters, and I have become free – freer than ever I would have been had I not had the redeeming experience of living here among them.

In saying such a thing it's easy to assume that he was being romantic about the poor. Was he living in the real world or just refusing to acknowledge the badly maintained housing, the dangerous street-life and the diabolical lack of amenities? For there is no getting away from the facts of life on one of today's council estates. They are often quite isolated places – even getting 'off' the estate to places of employment or to visit decent shops can be painfully difficult! The estates were often originally designed to make people stay put and look inward, in the hope that that would encourage tenants to bond with their neighbours and build community. But as with so many planning theories it had the opposite effect of cutting them off from the mainstream of the city's life. It also had the long-term effect of making those who do not live on the estate look upon those who do as an alien species. Naming the estate that you're from can often lose you a friend or, more frequently, the chance of a good job, a loan or a decent school place. So why did that young man say that living and ministering on the estate among such problems and poverty had set him free? It is precisely to that question that this book is hoping to offer an answer. So let's now try to pose this book's question in another way.

I was born and bred in the East End of London – not at that time known for its affluence! My parents were cockney, working-class people, who had known what it was to be really poor. They had both come through times of horrendous unemployment, and my father once mentioned that he had seen our mother starve herself in order that we children should not go hungry. But they were tough people for tough times – in fact, my mother was so tough that she is still going strong in her hundredth year! I was brought up in a very socialist climate by my family, especially by my Stalinist grandmother, but I always had the impression that my communist associates were being rather romantically biased about the poor working class and their ability to set the world right. As a young man, I warmed to their rhetoric, but in my heart I feared that if ever they took the reins of government the poor workers would fail just as badly as had the present ruling élite, or even, as in the Soviet Union, turn into a new élite themselves. But the question remained – what did some people think was so special about the poor that made my family believe that people like that could save the world? I read Karl Marx avidly in the hope of finding an answer and was fascinated to discover that Marx was in fact even more realistic about the degradations of the poor working class than even I was daring to be. In 1845 his close colleague Frederick Engels had published his study *The Condition of the Working Class in England* to show just how deprived and denigrated the poor had become. But despite that evidence Marx believed that there was still something about this left-out and abused proletariat that held the key to history. If only they would grasp it, he argued, they had the power to change society. But I was still not convinced that it would necessarily be a change for the better.

As our family continued to debate how the plight of ordinary people could be relieved, I searched in every corner for an answer to my uncertainties. I even ventured into the local church! And it was there that I heard my question framed in a way more stark and challenging than ever I could have imagined of such a conservative institution. It came at me right out of the pages of the Bible. St Luke is recounting the time when Jesus gave his masterly and authoritative sermon – the Beatitudes (Luke 6.20):

> Then fixing his eyes on his disciples he said:
> How blessed are you who are poor:
> the kingdom of God is yours.

So Jesus too was saying that the poor would inherit that better future for which we all yearned, but additionally he was declaring that even in their present condition they are blessed by God. Well, Jesus might have been saying that the poor are blessed, but they still did not look in any way blessed to me! This idea seemed insane. Yet I could not dismiss him as another pious romantic for it was very clear from all that I was reading and hearing about Jesus that he had been living with the poor of Palestine all his life, so he knew full well what poverty is and what it can do to people – how it can reduce and demean them; how it can isolate and de-skill them; how it can anger and even unhinge them – and still he was saying, given all his personal experience, that they are blessed!

All these years later I still struggle to know just what this saying of Jesus really does mean. And what's more, knowing the Church as I do, I am convinced that the Church at large needs to pay careful attention to this question if it is to become what it truly should be – the Christ-centred instrument of God's Kingdom, that his will might be done on earth as it is in heaven.

In the early months of 2011 I found myself confronted by more important decisions to make about my life. After 41 years of ordained ministry, it was time to retire and face the fresh challenges and opportunities that retirement would present. I wanted to devote what time remained to me to areas of interest that had been squeezed out by my daily round of responsibilities. There were three things in particular that I was looking forward to. First, I was strongly committed to a small charity, Friends of the Poor in South India, which I helped set up some years ago.[1] This interest takes me regularly to extremely poor areas of India, where I live with local Indian people who run the projects we support. This keeps me mindful of the intimacy of the global village in which we all now live and puts me in direct touch with some of the poorest people in the world. Second, I was pleased to continue as the Bishop Visitor to a convent of Anglican Benedictine nuns in West Malling in Kent,[2] where I meet regularly with the sisters to discuss their life of obedience and shared poverty. They are an enclosed order, devoting themselves absolutely to their relationship with Christ. Our conversations deepen my understanding of the value of the spiritual life and of the mysterious power of poverty and

1 www.fpsindia.btck.co.uk.

2 www.mallingabbey.org.

simplicity. Third, I was concerned to continue my commitment to those who live and minister on the poorest housing estates of Britain, and this was possible by virtue of my long-held membership of NECN, the National Estate Churches Network[3] – an ecumenical group of Christians who share my interest and concern for those very challenging areas. For many years, the Network had been a loose connection of friends, sharing regular newsletters and staging an annual gathering. But it had always lacked someone to travel the country, visiting its local groups in their own housing estate locations and gathering the stories of estate life and ministry today. So, by devoting a few days each month to journeying around the country I was given ample opportunity to listen to the poor on the housing estates as they shared their own experiences with me.

Through the first three years of retirement I therefore continued to visit India regularly, spent many hours deepening my understanding of convent life at the Abbey, and visited hundreds of people on poor housing estates up and down the country. And throughout this time, the common thread of all this activity – the question of poverty and this so-called 'blessedness of the poor' – was never far from my mind. I therefore determined to commit myself to a proper study of the question that had been dogging me throughout my ministry and which, God willing, I was now being given time and opportunity to address. But exactly how I was going to go about this, I was not entirely sure. Of one thing I was certain, and that was that I did not want to treat the question of poverty or the poor as some sort of abstract mind-game, for the intensity of suffering which I saw in the faces of those who were at the mercy of poverty told me that to have integrity, my question had to be grounded in the experiences of the people who knew most about it – the poor themselves. So often I had noticed that many books and reports on poverty limited their research to a discussion of what various scholars and researchers had said about the poverty data, and the poor themselves had only after that been asked to detail the wretchedness of their condition or to

3 www.nationalestatechurches.org.

specify what help they needed. But I had always believed that the poor should be the subject of their own history, not merely the object of other people's discussion about them. I wanted to begin and end my work therefore in the company of the poor.[4] This determination chimed in very well with the commitment I have had for many years to what we now call 'contextual theology', where a thoroughly incarnational method of study begins from a rootedness with the people in the place where the theological issue comes most sharply into focus.

Second, it was for me very important that we should not shirk the obscene reality of this subject matter by adopting a romantic view of poverty. I'd noticed that when I spoke to groups about Indian poverty, there was a tendency among my hearers to adopt this romantic approach – as if the Indian poor were rather exotic and endearing. But this reaction was never evident in my audiences when I spoke of the poor nearer home, here in the UK. Every culture has devised ways of ignoring or even downing upon the poor in their midst while honouring the heroism of the poor who are far away. In India itself, the poor are often believed to be poor as a consequence of a badly lived former life, so they are themselves to blame, while here in the secular UK we devise different arguments that allow us to arrive at a similar conclusion – that the poor are themselves to blame for their own poverty. I was keen therefore to concentrate upon the poverty that is near to home and to try to understand better the overlays of blame and antagonism that are rife in our culture.

Third, my discoveries about the recent history of poor housing estates in Britain was opening my eyes to a very concerning phenomenon which the sociologists are calling 'residualization'. It turns out that for a whole raft of reasons which we will go into later, our poorest housing estates have become places where our most needy citizens are now being crowded in together in a way that amplifies and multiplies the suffering that poverty causes. The *Independent* newspaper has gone so far as to say that today

4 Some UK sociologists have recently adopted this approach with remarkable success – for example, McKenzie 2015.

Britain's estates are 'social concentration camps'.[5] Some have likened this situation to the multiple deprivation of the old Victorian slums and rookeries in that we are now seeing in particular housing estates concentrations of poverty that have not been seen for generations.

Given these three concerns, it became clear to me that if I was going to understand why Jesus points us to the poor when he introduces the Kingdom, then it would be very instructive if I were to undertake my study alongside the people who live in Britain's poor housing estates. It would of course have been possible to focus upon rural poverty or the new poverty of the seaside towns and use those localities as case studies for a deeper understanding of poverty, but I have found that a concentration on social housing estate life sharpens the focus as no other perspective does. It remains one of the most challenging of all places in which to minister, it has none of the glitz and excitement of inner-city ministry to deflect our eye from the ball, and it is an area of life upon which a great deal of methodical and helpful sociological research has been recently centred. There is no doubt that intense poverty can be found in many hidden corners of Britain today, among the elderly, the infirm and the isolated, but on the poorest of our housing estates it is readily obvious, well-researched and, for me, easily accessible.

I am not the first, of course, and I will certainly not be the last, to write a theological book about the poor, and even in recent months new publications are finding their way to our libraries and bookstores. But my grave concern is that those publications mostly continue to treat the poor only as opportunities for those who are not poor to do their good works. The fine American scholar Gary A. Anderson, for example, has entitled his recent book *Charity: The Place of the Poor in the Biblical Tradition* (2013), as if to say that the Bible deems the place of the poor only to be objects of the

5 The *Independent*, Tuesday, 12 November 2013, stated: 'In England and Wales, the average electoral ward is 16 per cent public housing, but in the poorest wards that figure rises to 70 per cent or more. Britain's estates are social concentration camps.'

generous charity of others. There are also brilliant studies of the poor that offer new and exciting ways by which we can bring the gospel message to them, and others who major on how, by slimming down our consumption, we too can gain from the holiness of poverty. But while all these approaches have insights to offer, they remain somewhat limiting by treating the poor as the objects of our own interest rather than as the closest friends of Jesus. There are nevertheless theologians and practitioners who are currently thinking new things and wanting to start, as Jesus does, by being alongside and listening to what the poor themselves have to teach us. I hope that this book will be in that new tradition, offering a radical theology that is based upon what we learn from the poor, so that we can all go forward together. Perhaps then we will all be better placed to understand and respond to the pronouncement of Jesus when he declares: 'Blessed are you who are poor.'

I

Blessed Are the Poor?

A minister friend of mine who has lived on a very poor estate for some years describes his environment in the following way:

> The estate has many open spaces and was clearly designed to be an above average place to live. However, rents were too high for many ordinary people, and so the situation developed whereby people on housing benefit tended to be moved in. The estate has become one of the dumping grounds of the town. By one well-used statistical index it is the sixtieth most deprived area in England. Murders tend to be particularly violent, and quite a few are carried out by women. A recent arson attack saw a house completely destroyed, but fortunately the family were not injured. SRB [the government's Single Regeneration Budget] funding has been a big help. The last beat manager had excellent results, but now one beat manager is responsible for the whole estate and another difficult patch together. While there was money for estate caretakers, they made a big difference. One local activist made an impact over 15 years, but she died a few months ago. The local CSV [Community Service Volunteers] have two part-time workers on the estate as a result of a successful Lottery bid. That project has two years to run. The school achieves amazing results and employs many extremely dedicated staff. Many of the kids are poorly nourished and arrive hungry at school. They may not have a coat even for sub-zero conditions. A large percentage have to be self-reliant from an early age. Some even have parents who sell

> their kids' Ritalin prescriptions. A number born on the estate are never taken anywhere, even into the town centre.
>
> There has been a small congregation on the estate for about 33 years. It has never had a church building and always worshipped in community facilities. One vicar stayed for about 20 years and was a bit like their mother. People who worship here tend to be very poorly educated with some almost on the special needs level, but one of those disabled worshippers has a faith to shame us all, and I am very grateful she is here. Another estate, local to us, boasts a churchwarden with Down's syndrome. A group of evangelists who are connected with the Church of England has started work with local women and are running an Alpha club for kids after school. They are in the process of applying for CCF [Church and Community Fund] money. We are still looking for a way to work together. It's Jesus or bust on this estate.

There is no romanticism or glamour in his description, and yet he would not choose to live or work anywhere else. He later explained to me that after many years of committed, embedded experience in this deprived estate, he has grown so much to love the people he meets every day that he believes in his heart that Jesus is right to say they are blessed, but he is at a loss to articulate quite why. He certainly senses that the Jesus he meets in the Gospels would feel very much at home with these people.

Poverty in Galilee

The Galilee of Jesus' day was not, relatively, a poor region – indeed it was considered by the Romans to be an economically wealthy province due to its very fertile plain, the agricultural skills of its people and its advances in food technology, not least in the fish processing industry. But this wealth was not evenly distributed. Herod Antipas, in order to support his huge building programme, was taxing at a rate of between 25 and 40 per cent of both income and produce, which forced farmers to grow fewer crops for local consumption and produce instead crops that would raise a cash return. This left many local people hungry and drove many small farmers into debt, so that wealthy investors from abroad were easily able to buy out local farms. That meant that farm workers were now often labouring on land that they themselves had once owned, but which was now in the hands of absentee landlords. It was against this deeply felt sense of injustice that Jesus told such parables as that of the Vineyard Tenants and the Absent Landlord (Matt. 21.33–43). Likewise, while fishing on the Sea of Galilee had once been able to support lucrative family businesses like that of Zebedee and his sons (Mark 1.19–20), as a result of the eager competitiveness of the semi-globalization of the Roman Empire, the fish stocks were now being ruthlessly exploited and over-fished by foreign entrepreneurs using local day labourers. The fish were taken to the local factories in Magdala and other lakeside cities to manufacture salt-fish products, especially the Garum sauce which sold so well in Rome. Many Galilean fishermen were forced to sell up under such pressure and therefore had good reason to feel disaffected. As Jesus had occasion to observe, from the poor was taken what little they had, while the rich accrued even greater wealth (Luke 8.18).

Even from these few examples it becomes clear that many of Jesus' followers would therefore have been carrying the burden of significant poverty in relation to the comparative wealth of the region, their poverty resulting from the injustice and selfishness of the ruling wealthy élites. So when, in Luke 6, Jesus 'lifted up his eyes' towards them (v. 20) to tell them how the poor are blessed, he would have been gazing on people who could see wealth all around them but knew the injustice of having their share of that wealth only recently wrenched from their grasp. It would not have been difficult for them to discern the connections between wealth, poverty and injustice. By comparing much of Jesus' teaching with what we now know about the socio-economic conditions prevailing at the time, it is plain to see that he had deep and intimate knowledge of some of the motors that were generating the poverty around him, and he had personal experience of what that poverty could do to those being trapped within it. We see shades of this in his question to the crippled beggar who had lain by the Pool of Bethesda for 38 years. Here was a man who evidently could not afford assistance to help him into the health-giving waters. Before he heals him, Jesus asks him a telling question: 'Do you want to be healed?' (John 5.6, RSV) – Jesus was well aware that long-term destitution can make us apathetic and depressed, no longer able to take initiatives – even those that would be to our best advantage. Similarly, when four friends lower a paralysed man into the crowded room where Jesus was teaching, he is aware of all the issues of dependency that surround the situation. He heals the man and tells him it is time to take his life into his own hands and to take up his bed and walk (Mark 2.9–12). Jesus knew that the man should no longer be dependent on those who had always carried him. He needed empowerment as well as freedom from the immediate problem of his disability. And we too will be learning from Jesus that poverty entails a great deal more than the disabling absence of cash.

What exactly is poverty?

In order to listen attentively to the voices of poor people themselves, first let us clear the ground of some misunderstandings about the term 'poverty'. In today's world, there is often a distinction made between 'absolute' and 'relative' poverty – that is, the absolute poverty of those who are without the means of eking out even a bare existence, and the relative poverty of those who do not starve but are without the means to play a full part in their own society. Some believe that there is no real poverty in Britain, because only absolute poverty is of real consequence. They claim that only in places like India will you find absolute poverty, and I know to my shame what it is to walk past beggars on the streets of Delhi who have had both hands removed, so that they might attract the generosity of alms-givers! Around the world a child dies of poverty every four seconds, and almost a third of the population of our planet's population scrape a living on less than two dollars a day – the equivalent of about £1.20. But what makes the dire poverty of those Indian beggars so inexcusable is the complex relationship that their poverty has with the extreme wealth of others in that country. That wealth interconnects with their destitution. In other words, even their poverty is relative in that if the inequalities of the country were addressed, their abject poverty would subside and what is described by some as 'absolute' poverty would at last be recognized as relative poverty at its most cruel.

Similarly, sociologists here in the West recognize that while the UK is also assuredly a rich nation, here also there is a disproportionate distribution of that wealth to such a degree that many are unable to participate properly in society. At present five families in the UK together own more than the poorest fifth of the whole population. This leads us to realize that in fact all poverty is relative in so far as the wealth of the world is sufficient to support all its inhabitants if only it were shared justly. There is enough to fulfil everyone's need, but not to fulfil our greed. As we shall see, it becomes clear by studying the dynamics of poverty and wealth that poverty is more a measure of inequality than merely the absence of an income. We will see that this injustice was fully understood by Jesus when he observed it in Galilee, and it was this relational aspect of poverty that made it for him not only a matter of material concern but an affront to the justice that was essential to the Kingdom of God that he was inaugurating.

Social commentators have long talked of poverty as a dynamic and relational phenomenon. As far back as 1776 the economist Adam Smith argued that poverty is the inability to afford 'not only the commodities which are indispensably necessary for the support of life, but whatever the custom of the country renders it indecent for creditable people, even of the lowest order, to be without' (Smith 1776). By 1979 Peter Townsend was expressing what, 200 years after Smith, had become the consensus of Western opinion that individuals 'can be said to be in poverty when they lack the resources to obtain the types of diet, participate in the activities and have the living conditions and amenities which are customary, or are at least widely encouraged or approved, in the societies to which they belong' (Townsend 1979, p. 31).

For all practical purposes therefore, we can say that because economic development has progressed through the years in the UK, the problem at issue for us is not usually poverty in any absolute sense, although many cases of starvation and hypothermia do still come to light, but the constraining and debilitating effects of the inequality of opportunity, care and income which so contrasts with what the majority of our people would consider as basic and essential.

In recent years, the situation here in the UK has considerably worsened for the poor, because as our society has changed from a production-led economy into one where consumption dominates, those who do not have the wherewithal to engage fully in the consumer market because of lack of cash find themselves becoming increasingly irrelevant to our consumer society. In a consumer society, promises are made of more and more choices for its citizens, but those choices rely increasingly on a person's ability to purchase what's on offer. Similarly, in a consumer society even transport, education, health, housing and fuel are placed at the mercy of the market place, leaving the poor at a clear disadvantage, as they struggle more than most to find the money for basic essentials like prescription charges, heating and lighting, rent or the exorbitant interest charged by the credit companies who target the poor.

Calculating poverty

Once having realized that poverty is of this relational quality, governments have set about calculating where to draw the line between the poor and the non-poor. Here in Britain, this is usually done by calculating 60 per cent of the national average wage and counting those who fall below that marker as poor. In schools, we calculate that a child is in poverty if she or he has to be in receipt of free school meals for a period of more than six years. The weakness of a calculation of that sort is that when we talk about 'the poor' we fail to recognize that the reality is much more fluid, with families and individuals moving in and out of poverty as their circumstances worsen and improve. So for a child to be below the poverty line for six consecutive years means that that child is very impoverished indeed! Others therefore prefer to calculate how much income a household would currently require in order to meet a 'low cost but acceptable' budget for a selection of household goods. Campaigns are now well-established arguing that in order to protect against unforeseen events, if we add a margin of 15 per cent to that 'low cost but acceptable' budget, we arrive at a figure we can call a 'living wage' – an income sufficient to keep a family from slipping back into poverty.[1] It was as long ago as 1889 that Pope Leo XIII called for a similar calculation for what he called a 'just wage', justifying the calculation not simply on grounds of economic justice but on the basis of our shared humanity under God.[2] But now all these years later, for the first time in recent British history we find that although government figures indicate an upturn in the overall wealth and average income of our population, half of those living in poverty live in families where there is paid employment. They are working hard, but there is no justice in the amount they are paid. In other words, poverty is not just a problem for the poor but an indictment of us all.

We shall see evidence in this study that most of those in Britain who are poor enough to deserve welfare benefits are far too proud to claim them, which means that many are living even further below the calculated poverty line than statistics reveal. But it is also arguable that our system of welfare benefits and the way that system is administered is now unfit for purpose, and we also might ask if the benefits presently come anywhere near keeping beneficiaries above the poverty level. Given that the UK is still the fifth largest economy on earth, the astronomical rise in the numbers having to turn to foodbanks for survival proves that something is sadly amiss.

One of the things that we will quickly learn from our study of the Gospels and from coming alongside and listening carefully to

1 www.livingwage.org.uk.

2 Pope Leo XIII's 1889 encyclical letter *Rerum novarum* is now widely regarded as the cornerstone of Catholic Social Teaching.

the voices of the poor is that this lack of income is actually only one element in a whole combination of factors that truly make a person poor. The stories that they will tell will be of exclusion, loss of motivation and personal pride, of being made to feel guilty and ashamed, as well as lack of access to services like education, employment and health care. Poverty is a syndrome encompassing many symptoms and born of many causes.

For all the reasons I have described in my Introduction to this book, if we are to gain deeper insights into what constitutes poverty and why on earth Jesus called the poor blessed, it is best to do as Jesus did and get alongside poor people and learn directly from their experience rather than merely juggle statistics and think abstractly. And in Britain a very obvious place for us to look and learn from the poor is on our poorer housing estates, or housing 'schemes', as the Scots prefer to call them, for it is here that we will find all these issues writ large.

A distinctive shape

Housing estates are not like other urban areas and are very distinctive in many ways. To begin with, each estate is given its own name, either formally such as the Lansbury Estate in Poplar – named after its famous MP – or sometimes informally, such as the estate in Blackpool which the local police and social services have disparagingly tagged 'Baked Bean Island', since they assume that tenants there eat little else. Most estates are so distinctive that they are even easy to spot from the air. From that perspective it is very clear how different their formal planned design is from the urban sprawl of the suburbs or from the patchwork patterning of the inner city. The vast majority of our housing estates were actually designed to be different from, and often separate from, their surroundings. They are usually very well-defined areas in their own right, and any visitor walking the streets is easily able to tell when they have reached the edge of the estate, because the buildings will suddenly look very different; a main road may define its perimeter or perhaps the visitor will abruptly be confronted by countryside or a factory estate. The Belhus Park Estate in Essex was designed, like so many, with only one road in and out in order, so the planners insisted, to encourage tenants to look inward and create an internally cohesive community, but as so often has been the case elsewhere, this ploy actually isolated and alienated the estate from its surrounding communities.

Lynsey Hanley in her book *The Estates* (2007) makes a telling observation. From her own experience of growing up on a Birmingham estate she explains how the built-in confinement of the place, the inward-looking design of the estate, becomes internalized in the very psyche of those dwelling there. The wall around the estate, she says, is projected into the mind as 'a wall in the head' beyond which no estate dweller feels they can trespass: life is limited, horizons lowered, skills down-played. Ever since Plato wrote in his *Republic* of the ways in which the environment in which we are set can enhance or inhibit our clarity of mind, we have been aware how the built environment can impact our sense of wellbeing. We all know how a walk along the seashore can invigorate our bodies, calm our tensions and lift our horizons, but Hanley underscores how the confining and sometimes brutalizing environment of some of our estates can do just the reverse. The 'wall in the head' can send us inward and drastically limit our expectations of life and of ourselves.

On many of the older estates very tight and inward-looking family networks have grown up to compensate for that sense of isolation and vulnerability. And the need for such compensation is not an illusion. When set against the realities of severe loneliness or the dangers of violence, estate tenants very often do find themselves bereft of support and sanctuary, and it is for that reason that they build and value supportive networks, although unfortunately these can sometimes become negative subcultures resulting in aggressive tribalism and gang rivalry. Internal strife can also be the inadvertent result of the fact that so many homes of the same sort would have been built at the same time, so that people of the same generation all moved in simultaneously. This often led to strong relationships being established across the first parenting generation, especially during the child-rearing years, as mothers and children got to know one another at the school gates. But it left a rather lop-sided demography with no older generation to help care for the children. Then, as the children grew up and left home, the remnant generation grew older, and new families moved in to fill the vacancies. These families had different social needs and generational expectations, so that antagonism arose between the 'incomers' and the original inhabitants. Sociologists call this destabilizing process 'age-layering', a phenomenon that results in a community of extreme fluctuations, where suddenly there appears to be an overwhelming number of young people with the schools unable to cope, and a short time thereafter the schools empty, their parents become older, and there is a dearth of amenities to suit the elderly. Tensions and antagonisms arise, and those families who have the means seek stability elsewhere, leaving the estate to increasing tension and volatility.

The physical and psychological ghetto I've described can be made worse if the estate has become dismal and unkempt – and for many estates the environment is drab in the extreme. Gipton, the first 'garden suburb' estate in England, was built in 1935 and was deliberately designed without any local amenities but provided with a sparkling new tramway, intended to transport estate tenants to shops and employment in the centre of Leeds. Everything they required was available at the other end of the tram-ride. Over the course of years, however, the properties have been very poorly maintained, the roads allowed to decay, and the tram-tracks have been ripped out, leaving a wide tract of dreary dual carriageway through the estate which divides the community in two – and no new internal amenities have been provided to compensate, as is the case in numerous estates across Britain. Modern weekly shopping patterns require a family car or for the amenities and supermarket to be located nearby, but many old estates boast meagre car ownership and minimal amenities. Such is Gipton, but even modern estates seem to suffer the same fate. In 2001 a Baptist minister friend began renting a house on a newly built estate near Ashford – in the Thames Gateway regeneration area – and was told that shops and amenities were on track to arrive soon after. Nine years later the promised amenities arrived, but consisted only of a smelly fast-food take-away and a hairdresser. Most estates, new and old alike, boast a small row of shops somewhere within the neighbourhood, but on many of the older estates these shops have long been boarded up or shuttered, and if they do open, you shop there at your peril. Only betting shops, cheap pound shops and credit loan shops seem to thrive – with even the pubs now standing empty and desolate in their deserted car parks.

As if that were not enough, this drabness is also a feature of many an estate church building. Some are quite pleasant but suffer from dilapidation or design faults, while many others look like small grey concrete warehouses, made colder by broken-down heating installation, over-use of glass and substandard construction. Yet these worship spaces and halls are very often the only community spaces still functioning and available to the locals. Most remain down-at-heel and uninviting both inside and out, but occasionally a purpose-built or upgraded church will stand as a beacon of hope for the community – the congregation offering a warm welcome and substantial help to tenants and to one another.

As we'll see, from time to time through the years there has been a concerted effort to design and build well-appointed estates which still feel inviting and settled. Others have benefited from considerable injections of funds through regeneration schemes or have passed from local council ownership into the hands of tenants, private landlords or housing associations. As we'll learn, all this has made considerable impact upon the present scene and issued in a complex array of estates. But there remain, even where concerted efforts have been made, a very large number of estates where progress seems to have been minimal, and all too often the fabric, the environment and the standards of health and education have fallen far below anything that can be called acceptable in a country as wealthy as Britain. This sorry state of affairs is largely the outcome of a history of conflicting housing policies and political decisions that were intended to have altogether different consequences from what actually transpired.

A distinctive history

Perhaps it all started when the landed gentry of the sixteenth century built occasional cottages on their estates to house their farm labourers and retainers. But this 'estate housing' moved to an altogether different level when the Industrial Revolution took hold. In 1776 Richard Arkwright built his second cotton mill in Cromford in Shropshire, and to attract the 450 workers that he needed to operate the mill, he built in North Street the first row of industrial estate housing in the world. But as the Industrial Revolution went into overdrive vast numbers of workers were turned off the land, descended upon the towns and cities, and made to live in the pitiful homes that less principled managers than Arkwright provided for their workers. Over time, much of this accommodation was deemed to be so bad that government was forced to step in with its 1890 Housing of the Working Classes Act and, as a consequence, in 1900 the Boundary Estate was opened in London's Bethnal Green as arguably the first social housing scheme in the world to be built by a local government authority. The council housing estate as we know it had arrived.

The so-called Great War of 1914–18 forced the British government to acknowledge the miserable condition of the working class when a frightening percentage of volunteers for the trenches were found to be too sickly to sign on! Something had to be done about the disease-ridden slums from which they came. As the war dragged on, politicians such as Prime Minister Lloyd George promised the combatants that they would return to 'homes fit for heroes', but it was not until after World War Two that the building of council housing began in earnest. The newly elected Labour Party began building quality housing at an unprecedented rate under the keen eye of Nye Bevan, and when Harold Macmillan was elected as the very first Minister for Housing, he built no fewer than 300,000 new homes every year. Slum housing was cleared as the 1960s saw modern and none too reliable methods of concrete construction used to erect towering new blocks of flats across the sky-lines and around the fringes of our cities. The two major political parties outdid one another in their promises to build new homes and, by 1979, no less than 42 per cent of the population of Britain was housed in council housing.

But when in that same year Prime Minister Margaret Thatcher swept to power, she announced radically different policies on all fronts. As part of her drive to privatize the country's assets she introduced a flag-ship policy for council housing which promised all tenants the 'Right to Buy' their council house outright on astoundingly beneficial terms. The scheme proved very popular, and it soon became possible to spot the privately owned properties by their individuality and enhanced upkeep. As the years have elapsed, however, this same 'Right to Buy' scheme has produced unforeseen and very worrying consequences, not least the devastating fall in the number of homes remaining in local authority hands. These have had to be let to those people in most need so that many council housing estates, which once housed a healthy mix of families, have now become overwhelmed with very poor and needy tenants. Many an erstwhile diverse estate has become a sink estate for the unemployed and for those at the very bottom of the economic ladder – a phenomenon referred to as 'residualization'.

When Tony Blair was elected as the Prime Minister of a New Labour government in 1997, his Deputy Prime Minister John Prescott, like his Conservative predecessor Michael Heseltine, championed the regeneration of cities and towns using the new money that had become available as a result of the new competitiveness of globalization. Housing developers had a field-day, reaping heady profits by building vast estates of tiny houses and flats supported by very meagre infrastructure and few local amenities, but all stoked by banks offering ludicrously low-priced mortgages (Green and Baker 2008). This extraordinary availability of finance also funded a plethora of programmes designed to support the poor, and while that money lasted, great strides were made. But in 2008 the bubble burst, when the banks and financiers were no longer able to maintain the charade of ever-available credit, and the resultant economic recession bit into the poor more than any other group in society. Promised plans for new projects and better amenities were shelved, supports and benefits were withdrawn, and a new wave of unemployment sent even more people into abject poverty.

So it is that the history of social housing estates in Britain is a tale of innovation to meet need, residualization of the most needy, regeneration in times of boom, and destabilization of erstwhile secure communities. All this has served to escalate the traumas and uncertainties of an already poor and vulnerable population.

Distinctive people

Perhaps it is unemployment that currently most exacerbates the plight of the poor. In 1979 Britain boasted 7,000,000 manual workers employed in production industries, but by 2011 this had dropped to just 2,500,000, leaving vast swathes of working-class men and women unemployed. And with the demise of heavy industry, gone too were the unions that had, for all their faults, given a voice and a sense of community pride to the industrial workforce. When we consider how many of our housing estates were specifically built to house the manual workers of a local industry, we begin to appreciate what a devastating effect this about-turn in the economic order of our society had on those communities, with the relegation of a considerable number of them into very significant poverty.

Many housing estates are at the edges of our cities, but there are many too that are to be found at their heart. In these centrally located estates, more recent years have witnessed the process of gentrification rapidly taking place with altogether different consequences. Many of the old council properties were by now in the hands of housing associations, and private landlords who upgraded their inner-city properties and increased rents, forcing the poor out and attracting in the upwardly mobile. This allowed aspiring middle-class workers to live close to the exciting city centres where they could find office-based work and all the amenities the modern city affords. But the ousted poor had to go where they could.

In other old inner estates, many of those tenements which consisted of three- or four-bedroomed units were found to be well-suited to larger families from minority ethnic backgrounds. The large East London estate of Shadwell Gardens, for example, is now almost totally Bangladeshi, while in South London many house African or Afro-Caribbean households. This is so very different from the huge majority of outer-lying social housing estates elsewhere in Britain, where a visitor may walk for miles without ever seeing a person of colour. In most of the poorer outer estates across the country, it is still the old white working-class population that predominates, and you rarely come across a resident professional, save for the local vicar. And yet the one unifying factor across these estates, despite the differences of ethnicity, is the entrenched poverty.

Perhaps the worst conditions of all are to be found on those social housing estates that stand at an isolating distance from the city centres, for here tenants experience all the usual challenges of tough urban living – poor physical health, addictions, violence, gang culture, crime, mental ill-health, debt, poverty, ethnic tensions, and fear[3] – while in addition they face the isolation more usually associated with the rural poor. And for some it is that isolation which makes all the other problems eventually unbearable.

Demonizing the poor

When I am asked to talk about contemporary housing estate life to groups who have never experienced it, I often challenge the audience to play a little game with me. I ask them to shout out any words that come immediately to mind when I reveal the phrase that I have previously written on a large board. When I uncover the board they see the phrase 'Housing Estate', and on every occasion the audience has been embarrassed by its own response, involuntarily mouthing their unconscious associations – lazy, scroungers, lacking aspiration, obese, deprived. Rarely if ever comes a positive and complimentary word. The media repeatedly

3 See 'Area-Based Poverty', *Church Urban Fund Research Papers*, July 2011.

tell us that the poor are the authors of their own misery, and we have come to believe it.

Being diminished by poverty, no longer able to engage purposefully in our society because of unemployment, being hungry and reliant on foodbanks, housed in a vulnerable tenancy and with a drab environment for company – all this is bad enough for the poor, but added to these injuries is now the insult of being blamed for the poverty in which they find themselves trapped. 'Everyone is out to crucify us here, vicar!' observed one family whose combined wages were too low to sustain themselves without the assistance of state benefits and hand-outs. When you live on a council estate and are bombarded with insults of such intensity, it can play havoc with your self-image and interior peace, even if once you classed yourself as a reasonably robust personality. Even in casual conversation one hears blame regularly being heaped on the poor, and just recently I heard that at a local foodbank cat litter had been found in a donation of coffee.

How very different this demonizing portrayal of the poor is from that which we find in the Bible. Unlike our society, which labels the poor as loathsome and shameful, the Bible singles them out as God's special ones (Matt. 25.39). The Psalms and the Hebrew prophets testify that those who do not care diligently for the poor and the widow are deserving of hell's damnation (Ps. 14.4–6; Amos 8.6–7). Jesus spends his ministry at the service of the poor, taking every opportunity to be with them, to care for them and to make them his friends. And from that close encounter he is bold enough to say: 'Blessed are you who are poor.' What greater challenge could there be to the way our society is treating those who now live on our poorer housing estates?

The Church's response?

The Church has found itself extraordinarily blessed by the ministry of countless numbers of people through the years who have given their lives in serving alongside the poor on the housing estates of Britain. But more recently many of the denominational churches have withdrawn their support from the estates, deeming estate congregations financially non-viable. The influx of young cross-denominational groups has sometimes proved to be a great bonus while the Church of England, remaining true to its parochial tradition, still seeks to support a congregation in every area of the country, including the poorest estates. But all find it increasingly difficult. Some experienced ordained ministers clearly have more know-how and insight about housing estate life than any other professionals on the block, having lived and breathed it for so many years. Most are now alert to empowerment styles of leadership, encouraging laity to take the initiative in local community projects and to play significant roles in worship. Many congregations are finding that as government funding is withdrawn from local services and amenities, employees of these agencies are now queuing up at the door of the local church, asking to work in partnership in new and creative ways. It is clearly due to the commitment of the Christian Church that thousands of hungry people are now being fed from foodbanks across the country. Churches and church halls open their doors through the winter months to give shelter to the homeless, and no less than 22 per cent of Church of England congregations are sponsoring debt-counselling courses, and a fifth are supporting a local credit union.[4] Even larger numbers of congregations are keen to learn about poverty, its causes and its effects, and superb courses of study are being offered, not least that recently designed for Christians in the Rochester Anglican Diocese as their Lenten study for 2015 (Rochester 2015). For all these reasons many housing estate congregations are beginning to appreciate their own significance much more, both as an enduring, faithful presence and also as major players in the life of their community. And in harmony with this new engagement, fresh approaches to liturgy are being developed and new spiritual, biblical and theological insights spawned. Against all the odds there is a new spirit of excitement and purpose in some congregations, even in the most run-down poor estates.

4 www.cuf.org.uk/advent.

However, despite all this, it has to be acknowledged that the wider Church is mostly not yet up to speed with this new learning and experience in its midst. It is often still treating housing estate ministry as a peripheral after-thought. Evidence of this can be seen for example in the style and quality of the resources that it makes available to its estate churches. I have recently been taking time to visit many congregations and their leaders across the country, and I invariably ask them to recommend any Church-produced resources that they have found apposite for use among their estate congregations. Not once have I had a thoroughly positive response. 'We always have to change or re-work the resources that are offered to make them appropriate for our sort of people,' comes the answer. Many valiant local clergy and estate groups have devised their own materials and have allowed the wider Church to disseminate them, but really good resources are few and far between. Those that are good are usually produced by groups that are marginal to the mainstream, such as CURBS,[5] who produce wonderful materials for work with poor children, and UNLOCK,[6] whose biblical study resources are designed for those 'who can read but choose not to'. Likewise, church planting and church growth courses are available through the mainstream churches, but much more advanced and sophisticated programmes, more attuned to housing estate experience, are more likely to be offered by the cross-denominational groups who have much deeper and longer-term experience of these things.[7] The underlying cause of this mismatch seems to be simply that of class, for although the British have great difficulty understanding or defining what class is, nevertheless it is not at all difficult to see the disparity between the poor people of our estate churches and those who run and equip our denominations, and how that issues in such grave misunderstandings and mismatches. This is a contentious issue to which we must later return. It does mean, however, that even if church leaders are personally committed to

5 www.curbsproject.org.uk.
6 www.unlock-urban.org.uk.
7 See, for example, www.innerchange.org and http://eden-network.org.

the poor, for cultural and class reasons it may be very difficult indeed for them to know what to do about it. This is why Pope Francis has asked, in his very first Exhortation to the faithful, that we move not only towards becoming a Church *for* the poor, but a Church *of* the poor. He writes, 'I want a Church that is poor and for the poor. They have much to teach us' (Pope Francis 2013, § 198). By including the poor, listening to them and learning from them, the Church will be able to tread the path of Jesus who himself made the poor his constant companions. Only then may we begin to understand why Jesus calls the poor 'blessed'.

Listening to those at the edge

When we turn to the Bible, we find that it regularly tells us that it is the poor who will hold the key to our salvation. I continue to be fascinated and intrigued by a biblical story that is to be found in the second book of Kings, chapter 7. The scene is the city of Samaria, now under siege by the Syrian Ben-Hadad, the king of Aram. Elisha the prophet is concerned for the city's wellbeing, since it is said that its starving inhabitants are killing their own children for food! We learn that at the gate of the city there are four lepers, struck by such virulent skin disease that they are cast out of their own community. Being already on the edge of their society they debate among themselves whether they might try one last time to gain access to their city or whether they might wander into the camp of the besieging army to try their luck there. They know that they have nothing to lose, and because they are literally at death's door, they decide that they will risk all and see if the besieging army will offer them help. So they leave the specious safety of their own city gates and venture into the unknown – into the camp of King Ben-Hadad. But there they are confronted by a miracle. God had deluded the besieging army into thinking that the Egyptians had surrounded them, and so they had fled in the night, leaving the camp strewn with the wealth of all their belongings. The lepers are overjoyed and begin to loot the camp tent by tent. They eat and drink the fare and hide the booty. But then they are struck by remorse and say to one another: 'We are doing wrong. This is a day of good news, yet we are holding our tongues!' (v. 9). So they return and take the news of freedom back to the city. But the King is reluctant to receive the news, assuming it to be a ploy to entice the citizens out into the open. Eventually, however, it is discovered that these lepers from the very edge of society are indeed the carriers of the good news that will save the city, and the whole people stream out from the city to eat the food left by the retreating besiegers, leaving the King to wonder how it could possibly be that good news could come from ostracized lepers who had always been relegated to the very margins of society.

I find it illuminating to compare this ancient story with the teachings and actions of Jesus who time and again takes someone from the margins and places them in the centre, telling his followers to learn the Good News from them. In Mark 3.3 Jesus says to the sick man whose hand he is to cure: 'Get up and stand in the middle!' From the edge of the crowd he calls a little child: 'whom he set among them', and tells them to change and become like this child. He places a Samaritan at the centre of his story and an adulterous woman in the middle of the room. Just like the lepers of the story of the besieged city, these marginal people are the means by which the light dawns. Constantly, Jesus moves among those who are outcasts and at the edge of society in order to proclaim the Good News to the whole nation and inaugurate the Kingdom of God.

In the past, scholars assumed that Jesus spent so much time in the country villages rather than in the cities, because he preferred rural to urban living. Clearly, those early commentators had not been aware that the Galilee of Jesus' day was one of the most densely populated and urbanized regions of the Roman Empire. Overmann assures us that 'one could not live in any village of lower Galilee and escape the effects and ramifications of urbanization' (Green 2003, p. 21). These villages, often called 'cities' by the New Testament writers, were administratively connected to the powerful urban centres even though they were seen by the city élites as inferior, dependent and marginal. I am drawn to see many similarities between the villages of Jesus' Galilee and the poor outer estates of today – for, like our estates, those Galilean villages were struggling with the harsh challenges of life on the edge, prowled around by rival gangs and groups, pressured by the authorities, harangued by the politicians, beset by poverty and need, longing for a new tomorrow. This is the context within which Jesus operated and is the vivid backdrop to many of his stories and parables. And it was from this village base, on the margins, that Jesus then 'resolutely turned his face towards Jerusalem' (Luke 9.51), in order to confront there the heart of the matter – to bring the Good News from the peripheral and forgotten areas to the very centre of power in order to inaugurate a new beginning for humanity. It is within the context of the poor that Jesus frames his teaching about the Kingdom and, with them at his side, he brings it to bear upon the misshapen values of his contemporary culture. And in this way it is the poor who become the blessed vehicles of the gospel of his Kingdom.

If the Church of today can, like its master, live with the poor, learn from being among them, and bring their Good News to the centre of its own life, then a new day will have dawned, and it will be a sign of that same possibility for our whole society. As individuals too we will then have an opportunity to respond in a way that has integrity in the light of what we learn together. Pope Francis and the Archbishop of Canterbury are both urging us all to do just this, but I fancy that the Church at large will be alarmed at just how much change this will demand at the very heart of its culture. So it is imperative that we learn what Jesus meant when he told us to look to the blessedness of the poor as a key to his Kingdom. And for the Church in Britain the poor social housing estates are a good place to start on this journey of listening, learning and transformation.

2

Listening to the Poor

Listening to the stories

> Well, to tell the truth, we couldn't believe you was coming. We get lots of promises from the council and from the powers that be, but no one ever actually comes to hear what we've got to say. When you think about it, we've been living on this estate here for donkey's years, so we should know, shouldn't we? But no one wants to listen. So it's lovely that you're here. The vicar told us that you wanted to visit us, but we didn't really know what to expect. I mean, what is it you want to know?

The question was important, because when I visited poor people in their homes, in their churches and in community groups, I really did not want my own agenda to steer the conversations. I simply wanted to re-immerse myself in the experience of estate life and let the issues and questions begin to surface naturally from the people themselves. I did, however, have a clear notion of the overall method I wanted to adopt in order to get the very best from the conversations. It was a method that we helped to develop in the inner-city housing estate parish where I had been the vicar throughout the 1970s. I wrote up the full story of that experience in a little book called *Power to the Powerless* (Green 1987), and some time later I was encouraged to describe its methodology in greater detail in a second book entitled *Let's Do Theology* (Green 1990 and 2009). It is, in essence, a very simple process by which we first listen very attentively to people's vivid stories and experiences and share our own. After that, we look with more critical awareness at the issues that begin to emerge from that attentive listening. Then, when that is accomplished, we reflect upon those issues in the light of our Christian faith and gospel. And as that reflective interaction takes place there emerges a new vision of what God wants us to learn and what God wants us to do. It's a circular or cyclical process of learning that can be continued round again and again, forever carrying us forward into new depths of understanding and Christian witness. When I describe the method in this way, the process is apt to sound all rather clinical and contrived, but in fact it is simply a very natural dynamic of action and reflection. More than 40 years of practice has taught me that, without a doubt, it's the very best way to do theology. This is because it roots theology in God's world, which means: it is contextually based according to incarnational principles; it democratizes theology into the hands of ordinary Christians rather than containing it within the academies; and it results in commitment and response, which is essential if, as Jesus says, it is by our fruits that we will be judged as Christians (Matt. 7.20).

This action–reflection method of doing theology met with damning criticism from academics when I first wrote about it some 40 years ago. They argued that theology should be a wholly academic and intellectual exercise. I well remember one college principal, a specialist in Old Testament studies, accusing me with the words 'What, tell me, has politics got to do with the Old Testament?' But we have come a long way since then, and now most theological colleges and courses around the world offer studies in contextual theology along the lines of that early model – there is now even a Chinese translation of *Let's Do Theology*. But a very significant problem remains in that even among those who espouse or teach this method, few frame their own publications accordingly. It will, however, determine the shape of this book. First, we will listen carefully to the experiences of the poor themselves, told in their own words, and only then will we place alongside those experiences a more careful analysis of their predicament. Then pertinent connections will be made between the issues that emerge and the teachings and ministry of Jesus, together with the teaching of the Church through the ages. This will help us discern what the Church needs to learn from and with the poor and, as a consequence, what might be the right style of mission for us all to adopt as Christians.

So I invite you now to accompany me on this journey of discovery to learn what Jesus means when he says 'blessed are you who are poor'. We begin by listening to the poor telling their stories. I have by the way taken the precaution of changing some of the names and details so that people's privacy remains protected.

Hell or heaven?

Her flat was immaculately tidy and full of little mementos. Dotty and I sat at the little table in her kitchen. She liked sitting there, she told me, because from there she could see right across the green:

> It looks lovely from here, doesn't it? Very lovely. Those old trees must have been here for a long time. Just imagine what stories they could tell you. Longer than I've been here, and I moved in with my mum and dad in 1957. I was only a youngster really, and we were ever so excited. The place we came from wasn't all that nice – I don't suppose I remember it properly actually, because I was quite young. I was a teenager here on the estate, you see. Back then, I was so excited because they'd promised me a bedroom to myself and, well, I just couldn't believe it when I saw it. It seemed so big! I thought I'd just have a little cupboard I suppose but it was a proper room. Years later, when mum and dad went, I could have moved into their room, but I decided to stay put even when I got married – that was my dream room you see. We'd lived in a flat before, but it wasn't at all nice. All in the one room, and it was damp. All green lumps. I remember that! This place had all mod cons and hot water all the time – you're never cold here. You can even leave your windows open in the winter here. Oh yes . . . I married Andy. He was nice. I don't wear the ring now though. I don't know why, just don't feel right. He up and went in '73, just like that. It had

been brewing though. I don't think he ever liked this flat really. I thought it was big, when I was a nipper, but it's actually a bit tiny for a family, inn it? Perhaps that had something to do with it. Mind you I'd noticed too, 'cos when we first came with mum and dad like, it was lovely round here. Everyone looked after one another. I used to go to school – just over there look, you can see it from up here. But by the time Andy went, the whole estate had really got rough. It weren't nice. And as for the council, they didn't care what happened. Andy used to say that they were as bad as the gangs all round, 'cos no one ever came to check if you complained. It felt as if they thought that was what we deserved. I got angry I did. Mind you, it got even worse later on. Kids were messing with all the cars and you really didn't feel safe. Not that I'd go to the local shops actually – it's all past 'best before' stuff there, and it's no cheaper than proper shops. I had a little car for a bit and that made life so much easier. But I had to give it up. But back then it was absolutely awful. You could even see the drugs, but the police said that they wanted to keep the drug people in one place, so they could keep an eye on them. Well, why couldn't the police take them off to their own street and keep an eye on them there? – that's what I said. They couldn't do anything, or they didn't want to. They took over some flats and the noise of all the shouting and screaming, it was awful. You couldn't get to sleep. I don't know what it is but all that seems to have got a lot better recently. I've even spoken to the kids in one little gang who wait around the bus stop – I use the bus to go to my little cleaning job. Those kids are lovely, just larking about but not making trouble. No jobs for them though. I said: 'you should do a cleaning job like I do', but they didn't want to know. Just laughed. Fair enough I suppose – it's not a job for a strong lad. He'd feel silly doing my job. Anyway, it don't pay enough. Do you know the worse thing? I go to work and I work hard too! But it's still not enough to live on. The worse thing was going to the foodbank. Well, I didn't actually go in in the end. I look after Clare's kiddies weekends, and one weekend I'd got nothing – and I mean nothing. I don't drink – I do smoke I'll admit that, but not even ten a day. And I'd got to the end of the week, and didn't have no food in the house. I know where the foodbank is, so I went along but I felt so horrible I couldn't go in. I got all weepy in the street and had to come home. I couldn't go in there. I'm not one of them. I had to tell Clare I couldn't have the kids. My one chance in the week to see 'em, and I had to miss it. Never used to be like that – if you had a job, you could afford to feed your kids! I wouldn't leave here though. I like it round here now. I mean, it wouldn't make no difference about my money if I lived somewhere else, would it? I know this estate too well. Wouldn't leave. I've got memories, you see. Do you want a top-up? There's more in the pot!

Who cares?

The little wooden gate swung on rather rusty hinges as I followed the vicar up the garden path to an open front door from which issued laughter and banging. The tiny rooms were dark and crowded, but Joan, dressed in overalls and heavy duty rubber gloves, gave us a royal welcome. 'It's coming on!' The occupants of this very small terraced house had been in great trouble with the police, the husband having been accused of a serious crime – even the neighbours had taken against them, and someone had trashed their home. But other friends had decided to clean up the house and give them a welcome on their return. There was no proper furniture to be seen anywhere – just bare floorboards, three plastic-topped stools and a work surface in the kitchen. Three or four young men were struggling with an overflowing downpipe in the overgrown back garden, while the women hustled around for a cup and some milk. 'We've painted up the bedrooms upstairs, and we've had a wash round down here, look. It's not much but I think they'll like it when they get back tomorrow. There's even a bed upstairs. 'Ere, look here! That's their pet rat in there. I wouldn't want one, would you? They say it's good company, but I don't see that – do you,

Fiona? Bad enough having a rat for a husband!' 'Oi, you behave yourselves in there and get us another cuppa tea, this downpipe stinks.' The banter was cheering and, despite the mess and paint pots dripping across the floor, the atmosphere was warm and welcoming. 'You'd have thought that with that young couple being so badly treated that the Council would at least have done something to make this place liveable in!' Just a few neighbourly friends had rallied round, despite the antagonism of others, to do what they could to help a couple in real need – whatever they might or might not have done. It was an experience that I was to meet time and again – the determination to help others when they had hit rock bottom, right or wrong.

The quest for security

The final home visit of the day was to see Harry and Debs, a young couple with two children. The front door was open but no one seemed to be home. We shouted through, and Harry shouted back: 'She's gone in next-door for the bab.' Debs soon arrived with their two children in tow, the seven-year-old boy full of energy and struggling to run off, while the baby girl slept on her mother's shoulder. 'We thought you weren't coming after all, and now the kids are back. How are you, Father?' 'I'll play with Jack in the front garden, and you can chat to Bishop Laurie, how's that?' I entered the front lobby, stepping over a rough pile of what looked like rags, old clothes and toys and on into the downstairs room. Harry sat in the corner on the one upright chair, turning now and again to finger his computer keyboard as Debs went off to make up orange squash for us all. She was soon back with us, sitting at Harry's feet on the floor, sipping at her squash. I sat on the small sofa just inside the door, while against the far wall was a jumbled pile of plastic toys and under the window an enormous free-standing television of the old-fashioned sort. The walls were not decorated, but for some reason a wide black line had been painted all around the room at shoulder level. The muddle and disorder evident around the room seemed to be a mirror image of the chaos that had so surrounded their lives. Debs did all the talking:

> See, what happened – oo, what do I call you? Can we call you 'Father' as well? Well, what happened, Father, is that we've been moving from place to place trying to get a place that was big enough. We've had horrible landlords – one got me really scared, when I said that he was charging too much. It was only one small room, and we shared a kitchen and toilet with the other families, and there's four of us. We tried everything, but nobody listened. We even went to the church, but they didn't want to know us. Then I met Father Paul, and he listened to us. It was great. He really did listen too. So we got this place with his help, but then I got frightened again, because there was funny things. It got really aggressive with me and knocked me about. So Father Paul came and talked with us, and he said all these prayers round the house, and it all seems different now. I still hear the noises but I'm not frightened any more. No one else ever bothered with us, we was all by ourselves just being pushed around, but it's not like that anymore. It's not all over but we're doing all right, ain't we, Harry? Are we poor? Well, we ain't got enough to live on, if that's what you mean. We have to get things where we can. He's out of work, but he does little jobs when he can get them, and that helps out. Putting up shelves for people last week, you know. The church people have helped – got us this pram. We've come to church an' all, and it was great. I was frightened that they wouldn't like the kids, but they've been lovely, especially the old people. We're all going to be christened in two weeks. They're giving us a party! That'll be nice, Harry, won't it?

Few expectations?

So often on my travels I would visit the estate primary school, and invariably I was impressed by what I saw. 'There's a glass ceiling for these children,' said one head teacher, sitting in her office surrounded by garishly coloured teddy bears:

> I consider it my job to convince the parents just how talented their children are. I think they are sometimes a little scared themselves of the fact that their children might be very able. But coming from this estate, I know that when they go on to the comprehensive, they'll just be lost in the crowd, if the teachers are not alert to how talented they are. It's expected that these children will be failures, and I have to tell their new teachers they're not. My staff need to have the usual teaching skills but also a problem-solving talent, because every day there will be something. I've got a great team, they look after one another, and, of course, in the end, as hard as it all is, it's the children themselves who sustain you. Of course, if one of my teachers does find the strain too much, we have proper support for them. I have to undertake risk and stress assessments for each post, and we have a very good supervision team who counsel our staff on work–life balance, emotional health and wellbeing. They do that for all the estate schools across the city.

As we left, I explained that we rarely have anything like that in our churches for ministers who find the going hard. She smiled, gave me a big hug, and said: 'Well, go and set it up then!'

Where's home?

Not only are social housing estates different one from another, but also it would be a grave error to assume that each person on one estate is the same as the next. Mercy's story was distinctive, and yet shared some similarities with many of her generation:

> I had a good education in Nigeria – I come from Enugu, and although my parents were not wealthy, I went to the Roman Catholic school, and my mother wanted me to train as a nurse.

She trained as a nurse there years ago. But I had other ideas. I loved to sing in church, and I joined the choir and sang a lot in school. It was difficult for me, when I told my mom that I wanted to become a professional singer. In high school I did OK. I fitted in OK but always felt I was trapped somehow. It wasn't easy for me. So I said to my mom that I wanted to go to England to make a better life for myself. They didn't want it, but eventually, I don't know how it was arranged, but I came and lived with my auntie in Nottingham. That was in 1997. It was very difficult for me, because I did not understand the culture. Some places looked all right, but most places were not at all like the picture of England I had had in my mind. It was very cold – I was freezing most of the time! – but the people seemed so cold to me too. But everything was new for me, so I had a good time anyway. At first, the only friends I had were from my auntie's family, but then in church and choirs I made new friends, and life got better for me. But in those early years I was very lonely. Eventually I got this flat with a friend. It's very small and not very nice really, but it's ours. The landlord is never here, but my friend, he's good at repairs, so we just get on with it.

In Nigeria we all live very close together, but here everyone is separated. It took me a long time. I had some problems last year. You see, when people ask me here, if I feel Africa is my home, I say that it is for sure. But I went back last year, and then I found I did not really feel I belonged there any more. Even though my little girl is there, it all felt very strange to me. It's all so restricted and I found I could not talk very freely to my old friends. My mom felt very distant, and that made me sad, you know. So I guess I have to say now that I'm more British than African – no, I can't say that. That would be stupid. So I don't know what to say now. Makes me feel a bit lonely not being sure. I like it here though. I didn't get anywhere with my singing, and I had to write to my mom to tell her I was going to train to be a nurse after all. She liked that. Now I work in A&E. It's very hard work, but it's very rewarding, and I think it is God's will for me, so I'm happy enough. There are lots of black people on this estate, but most of my Nigerian friends live on the other side of the town – not too far though. I'm still with them a lot, but my church life is the most important thing for me now, and my church is here on this estate. It's a bit traditional, you know, and we have to share our priest, but the people are lovely. We even put on a musical, *Joseph and the Technicolor Dreamcoat*, and I had a part – but the funny thing is, I was Joseph! They said I had the strongest voice! Isn't that funny? But I loved it. Most of them are white, but they're all right really. They're quite nice actually!

Where's the work gone?

One of my visits took me to Newcastle, once a world centre for ship-building. But now the high price-tags in the city centre shops and the elevated house prices were at odds with the grinding poverty of so many of the people on the surrounding social housing estates. Reece and his father before him had worked in the ship-building industry – both highly skilled manual workers. He had managed to keep his job when many of his friends were being laid off, but eventually the cancer of unemployment hit him too, and although he had tried repeatedly, no prospective employer favoured him over the many other men who offered similar redundant skills. He had despaired and started to drink heavily, which in turn led to his wife teaming up with another man, leaving Reece without his children and his car. 'I met Kelly one night when I'd had a skin-full. She sorted me out and made me feel like a man again.' She also supplied him with a ready-made family of five of whom he was now inordinately proud. His stepson Frankie, on leaving school, had been hopeful of an apprenticeship, but there were none to be had. 'I wonder if them apprenticeships are any good anyway any more. You know, they only get £2.50 an hour as a young apprentice. And at the end of the training he could end up like me – skilled and still no job!'[1]

1 Pay for apprentices aged 16–18 now stands at £2.70 per hour according to www.govt.uk/apprenticeships.

Reece and Kelly are managing on a small budget by purchasing goods which clearly have a rather suspect provenance:

> I know where the stuff comes from, but when they come round door to door, the low prices help to make ends meet. Lots of local families depend on it. We've all become regular customers. And I don't mind telling you, I claim all the benefits I can. I've paid National Insurance contributions all my working life to guard against a situation like this. I mean, if you paid for any other insurance, and then when something went wrong the company didn't pay up, you'd be able to take them to court, wouldn't you? If there was work out there, I'd be at the front of the queue, I can tell you. I love working.

Both Reece and Kelly are very resentful of immigrants from Eastern Europe, who they claim are supported by the welfare state, when they have not contributed. 'What I can't understand', says Reece, 'is why they sent all the industry abroad. If there's no industry, what can the working man do to feed his family? So it's the government's fault for being so short-sighted, and that's why the government owes me. It wasn't me who closed down all the bloody factories.' When it is argued that it was not Thatcher's government that shrank British manufacturing industry but global financial forces, Reece gets angry and asks:

> If she [Prime Minister Margaret Thatcher] was forced to do it, how come it didn't force Germany to get rid of all their industry then? They're still pumping out cars and making a fortune, and we've got nothing left to make our fortune with! All these streets were built so everyone could walk down to the shipyard, where we all worked together. Now all that's gone, and the heart's gone out of it all. Same in the mining villages. The new jobs on offer are miles away and don't suit me anyway. It's all either paperwork or sitting in front of a screen, or else it's security – walking round in a uniform telling kids to get out of the shop. They tell us to go where the work is, but why should we say goodbye to all our family and mates and things? But I

tell you I'd like to see their faces down in Westminster if a couple of thousand Geordies all turned up at their job centre and queued up for their jobs! That'd teach them to tell us we're lazy!

Nothing much to live for?

It was on a run-down estate in Birmingham that I found myself chatting with a group of young 'hoodies', who were sheltering from the rain in an old disused garage. In a society like ours, where to participate requires cash, these boys were inevitably marginal simply because they had no money in their pockets. I found that groups of youngsters would talk with me for hours, if I offered to buy them a burger – they were simply broke and very hungry. 'You can't get a job you know – and I'm prepared to do anything I am – anything! And you know what? If you get a job, the wages are useless. I don't play their game. I can get more money by just nicking it.' Advertisements for young people's clothing, software and leisure, together with peer pressure, prove an irresistible lure, but how do the lads I met have any chance of fulfilling those dreams? To achieve academically when your starting point is so low takes exceptional intellectual talent. I asked them about school, and their responses were anything but positive. 'School's just like a prison with lots of stupid rules. I make my own rules I do.' Some youngsters I'd met elsewhere had spoken very positively about their school, but I sensed that they had firm support in that from home. These lads did not. One lanky boy with frizzled hair told me that his sister had done well at school but was now working on the check-out in the same supermarket where he already had a job gathering up the shopping trolleys. 'It didn't do her any good. Her pay's no better than mine – and that's puke. She's stuck indoors on the till – at least I can have a lark outside.' He and his sister were both on part-time minimal wages, not a living wage, and it was clear to me that their combined income would not buy their way into any reasonable standard of living. Some of the more enterprising youngsters therefore ran their own money-making schemes as DJs or car cleaners, and one young woman was making her way in a singing group, but often their considerable entrepreneurial skills were used illegally. And where there was crime, there lurked the inevitability of attendant drugs. Each of them boasted that they had used drugs, although I knew from my own gang experience that you could never be sure how much of their response was bravado to impress their peers. 'Getting skunk is easy. It's everywhere you look. You can make a lot more money buying and selling the better stuff – or even dealing the rubbish! And there's loads of duty-free about too if you know where to go.' My own wife had once felt rather naïve when, on visiting a local family home, she asked: 'Oh, you're getting ready for Christmas then?' and was met with a glazed stare. She immediately realized that the house was piled high with duty-free liquor and cigarettes for resale.

Many of the estate youngsters I talked with felt that society had nothing for them, and that being the case, their main concern was to get as much excitement into their lives as they could in other ways:

> We know what's right and wrong but we don't do it. Doing the wrong thing gives you a high. Doing the right thing doesn't give you the buzz, does it? Best thing is doing things together so everyone sees. Look at this! Rocko made this video of hitting this stupid guy, and it went viral! But what I like is doing TWOCking [taking cars without owner's consent]. Get a good car, then drive round with the windows down and shout at other gangs. Awesome!

When these same young people were by themselves for a moment they seemed, however, altogether different and would share their hopes for a partner, a family with children, a car and a home. But they had already made the calculation that it was an impossible dream. As they grew older, many would spend their time in the ubiquitous betting shops, which held out the forlorn hope of a good win to liberate them from their lacklustre lives – and even a betting loss could offer a moment of animation and alleviation from the boredom of living in this grim place.

The sheer strain of it all

Christine and Jacko were very frightened. 'We won't be able to afford this. And it's not our fault we've got spare bedrooms – they're only little box rooms anyway. But if we lose those, where will our kids go when they come to stay? Bang goes our Christmas with no kids around!' The so-called Bedroom Tax imposes a loss of 14 per cent of benefit income value if a household has one spare bedroom, or 25 per cent if it has two or more spare bedrooms:

> If we can't manage, they say we've got to move out but where to? The only friends we've got live round here, and all the houses have got spare bedrooms. We've lived here all our lives – it'll kill Christine! The Council say they've got no smaller ones for us anyway, so we've got to stay where we are. Where are we going to get money like that with this Bedroom Tax?

Logic dictates that this tax will prove unworkable and will have to be changed, but its very existence is indicative of the fact that those who are designing policy are totally out of touch with the realities of the poor – and don't understand how their decisions will affect vulnerable people. But this is not all. The abolition of the Council Tax Benefit and the requirement that benefit claimants now pay a proportion of their Council Tax from their present incomes makes many lives unsustainable, when they are already scarcely making ends meet. If an adult has to live on unemployment benefit at £72.40[2] a week, how would they be able to pay the additional 8.5 per cent to 20 per cent of the Council Tax that local authorities are wanting to demand? As I write, government cuts are eating into the lives of the poorest in a way that the richer sections of our society could hardly comprehend. Most claimants receive nothing like the maximum entitlements, but for those who are in real trouble and have to claim housing benefit there is now the 'benefits cap' of £350 a week for a couple without children

2 www.gov.uk/job-seekers-allowance/what-you'll-get.

and £500 a week for couples with children. For many of those still living in the now gentrified pockets of the south of England, where rents and costs have been escalating so wildly, the new caps and sanctions are forcing poor families to move away from their support networks and what meagre employment they may have. The elderly poor are particularly vulnerable.

Worry about money can even undermine erstwhile resilient individuals and their families, and some households find themselves having to carry someone whose mental stability has been shattered by debt and worry. Christians Against Poverty is a growing national network who report that no less than a third of those who contact them about debt are suicidal. One man records that he cried with relief when the debt counsellor had made a visit – 'someone at last had listened and given me my future back'. The journalist Lynsey Hanley (2007, p. 165) draws our attention to cortisol, the hormone that the body produces in times of stress. She tells us that cortisol is beneficial for the body, as long as it is discharged in small doses, but if the body is called upon to produce it for extended periods, as it is for those living under the hammer of prolonged debt, it can be overwhelming and result in the weakening of the body's immune system and essential organs. No wonder the poor find themselves having to cope with higher rates of physical illness than others, given that they are forced to contend with the long-term presence of cortisol to help them contain their stress. A very interesting research project showed that taken together, the many associated stresses of living in social housing have extraordinarily long-term effects. In 2009 the Tenant Services Authority, the Joseph Rowntree Foundation and the Scottish government joined forces to publish a joint report (Lupton *et al.* 2009), which stated among its key findings:

> On average, those who lived in social housing as children were worse off as adults in terms of health, well-being, education and employment than their peers . . . For each generation and every measure we used, those who had ever been in social housing in childhood fared worse as adults.

It was notable that, as thorough as they were, the investigators were never able to find an area of concern where those who had lived in social housing did better than those who had not. When I think back to my conversations with those young people on the street, it seems to me that the negative assumptions they had about their future prospects were probably going to prove accurate. For them, life would be an uphill struggle and their secret dreams would never be fulfilled.

It's all the fault of the poor

In this chapter we have been listening to the voices of those who live on some of the poorest housing estates in Britain. There has only been space to record a tiny fraction of my many conversations and encounters – some of which I must admit have been very harrowing. But it is also important to reflect upon what others say about the poor – and this is a voice that, unlike the voice of the poor, is heard so constantly and so stridently that it has now become commonplace talk in day-to-day conversation and is often provoked and reinforced by our newspapers and politicians.[3] This demonizing of the poor has become so disagreeable in recent years that a number of national churches have together published a report intended to put an end to these unpalatable and divisive fictions. The report (Baptist Union of Great Britain 2013) looked at six of the most common of these myths, showing in each case how they run counter to the facts.

The first misconception, that *the poor are lazy and don't want to work*, is readily dispelled when we realize that poverty in work is now more common than poverty out of work. The majority of the poor are in employment but don't receive a living wage. The report tells us: 'Excluding pensioners, there are 6.1 million people in families in work living in poverty compared with 5.1 million people from workless households' (p. 13), and the majority of children in poverty hale from 'in work' households! Among those

3 See, for example, www.number10.gov.uk/news/troubled-families-speech.

deemed to be 'employed' we find as many as 1,400,000 people who are forced to work far fewer hours than they need in order to gain a living wage. And all this is even in the face of what Winston Churchill said in 1909 when he was President of the Board of Trade: 'It is a serious national evil that any class of His Majesty's subjects should receive less than a living wage in return for their utmost exertions' (Hansard, 2 April 1909).

A myth is also circulating that the 5.1 million poor who live in workless households are led by those who simply *prefer to live on benefits*. Yet over the last 30 years the value of the benefits has halved relative to average incomes (Oxfam 2012), which means that the standard of living for claimants is now at a distressingly low level. Most who claim out-of-work benefits turn out to be either sick or disabled, and after that come those who have been made unemployed and are actively seeking work. To receive Universal Credit or Jobseeker's Allowance they must demonstrate that they have only minimal savings, and have been searching diligently for work and undertaking any training that the Job Centre adviser believes will be helpful. If they are assessed as having a disability that precludes immediate work, they are still required to undertake tasks to prepare for work, and then undergo at least an annual reassessment of their condition which we're told can prove quite humiliating (Spartacus Network of Disability Researchers and Campaigners 2012). If anyone seeking these benefits fails to fill in the complex paperwork correctly, turns up for an appointment even ten minutes late, or fails to work on job applications for the required number of days per week (including Christmas Day), then they are sanctioned, which means that they receive no benefit at all for a set period, which can mean a family receiving no help *whatsoever* for up to three years! This is the primary cause of the sudden increase in queues at the charity foodbanks (BBC 2012). It is hard to understand why anyone could believe this myth that living on benefit is an easy option.

That *the poor are addicted to drink and drugs* is unfortunately a myth that church-goers as much as the rest of the population believe to be true (Church Urban Fund 2012a). Again, the report points out that only 4 per cent of claimants for the main out-of-work benefits are receiving them as a consequence of the misuse of drugs or alcohol (Government 2012), whereas we know that alcohol consumption increases greatly as you go up the income scale, not down it, with no less than 9 per cent of British men being estimated by the NHS to be symptomatic alcoholics. As horrendous as the national figures are across the board, drug and alcohol abuse are simply not major causes of benefit claims.

Almost half of the nation's population believe that the poor would not be poor if they learned to *manage their money more carefully* (Bamfield and Horton 2009). But imagine yourself, for a moment, living on an unemployment benefit of £72.40, contending with the national hike in electricity bills, the astronomical increase in basic food prices, and without any savings for a rainy day. I doubt whether many of those who accuse the poor of being careless with money could budget as well as those who manage on this income. Similarly, many believe the poor let the size of their family get out of control, but again statistics show no difference in family size across the socio-economic spectrum.

The next myth goes for the jugular. In surveys (Government 2013), between 80 and 90 per cent of citizens accuse the poor of approaching the benefit system with *criminal intent*, fiddling large sums by fraudulent means. It has not been helped by the statement of George Osborne, the Chancellor of the Exchequer, in the House of Commons on 20 October 2010 that 'we estimate that £5 billion is being lost this way [through benefit fraud] each year'. This was a statement that proved so entirely false that his department had later to amend it (Government 2010). He had added in all the government errors, masking the fact that the actual amount of the welfare budget lost through fraud is at an all-time low, no more than 0.9 per cent (Government 2013). It would be naïve to think that no claimants at all were 'on the fiddle', but on the other hand if all those who did deserve benefits were prepared to go through the humiliating process of claiming them, the welfare bill would be £18 billion more per annum than it currently is. An astonishing figure! Pressure is on from many quarters to buy into this myth of false claims, and the government spends a lot of money advertising its hotline specifically designed to help neighbours alert tax officials to any suspected fraud. The hotline receives a quarter of a million calls a year, and yet only a fifth of those calls are deemed to have sufficient substance even to warrant investigation, and of those that do, less than a tenth are found to have claimed too much[4] – and given the complexity of the claims forms many of those cases are found to be errors of calculation on the part of claimants rather than any intention to defraud.

The final myth the report attacks is that the poor *brought the economic crisis upon Britain* by escalating the costs of the welfare budget. This was clearly stated by Iain Duncan Smith, the Work and Pensions Secretary, in the *Today* programme on 14 June 2012. The truth, however, is that over the past 20 years the proportion of government spending on welfare has remained surprisingly constant, only rising after the banking crisis of 2008, which resulted in so much unemployment. However, it is worth noting that the Baptist Union report calculates that the amount the government then spent on Quantitative Easing, a policy designed to slow the recession and that increased the wealth of the country's richest fifth of families, could have paid the full cost of Jobseeker's Allowance for over 100 years (Aldridge *et al.* 2012). The cuts have been bad enough, but blaming the poor for their own poverty is the unkindest cut of all.

It is important for the Church to play its part in dispelling these baseless myths, but in doing so it should not adopt an over-romanticized view of those in poverty. Poor people will often believe these same myths themselves, but direct them at immigrants and others who are outside their immediate circle of friends and family. In this regard, they are no better nor worse than the rest of the population. And, of course, there are thieves and scroungers among the poor just as among the non-poor, the only difference being that the financial gains for the rich tax evader are in a league all of their own. Poor people are also as guilty as other human beings are of projection – accusing others

4 House of Commons written answers, Hansard, 5 April 2011: Column 748W and 7 March 2011: Column 858W.

of faults that actually lie hidden within ourselves. Some indulge in aggressive behaviour too – although the non-poor often have opportunities at work and elsewhere to give vent to aggression in ways that are more socially acceptable or even applauded within the competitive business culture. But there is probably not much to choose between any segments of the population when it comes to righteousness. Jesus knew this all too well and never romanticized about the poor. It was not lack of realism that made him look directly at the poor and call them blessed.

No voice for the poor?

We have been hearing some of the disparaging myths about the poor that have become so commonplace that even the poor themselves have begun to buy into the fiction that no one is to blame for their poverty but themselves. Hearing these voices emanating constantly from politicians and the press and recapitulated time and again in common conversation serves only to blunt a person's aspiration to better themselves or to continue their relentless struggle against the odds. But the resilience of the poor always strikes me as extraordinary, as they manage from day to day on such meagre resources and the promise of a worse tomorrow. We hear reports when youngsters become aggressive on the streets or when neighbours turn nasty, but given the injustice that they daily experience, it seems odd that we don't actually hear the poor's own side of the story very much at all. There are four major reasons for this. First, managing on so little is exhausting, leaving *scant reserves of energy to campaign* or organize to make their concerns heard. Second, with the fall of the Berlin Wall in 1989 came *the collapse of the language* of socialism by means of which many of the concerns of the poor had been identified, named and analysed. I remember growing up in an atmosphere where working people would discuss their plight together and seek to understand the pros and cons of the economic and political system they served. There was an abundance of clubs, pubs and societies where such conversations could take place, and the vocabulary of socialism served as a vehicle for debate, even for those workers who discounted the socialist theories that attached to the language. But the West was quick to interpret the fall of the Berlin Wall as a justification for dismantling the very language of socialism; and without a language on which to hang ideas, human beings can no longer organize their thoughts let alone analyse a situation and formulate responses.

Third, as socialism was systematically discounted, the language that thereafter prevailed was that of the unregulated *market place of competition* – 'winners and losers', 'every man for himself', and other unsavoury phrases. Gone were concepts of solidarity, cooperative endeavour, or united action. Simon Blackburn reminds us in his book *Mirror, Mirror: The Uses and Abuses of Self-love* (2014) that the phrase 'greed is good', which soon gained common currency and accused the poor of being weak and unimaginative, was only coined as late as 1987 in a satirical film called simply *Wall Street*.[5] Before that, in 1981 an influential business magazine announced that 'corporations have a responsibility, first of all, to make available to the public quality goods and services at fair prices . . . the long-term viability of a corporation depends upon its responsibility to the society of which it is a part'. By 1997 the same organization stated that 'the principal objective of a business enterprise is to generate economic returns to its owners' (Gomory and Sylla 2013, p. 109). This complete about-turn in language and mindset seeped into the common understandings of ordinary people across the globalizing world so that most of those who are now under 40 have not even heard of the values with which an older generation grew up. As the market was allowed to become the dominant factor in so much of our thinking, very suddenly the poor were deemed to be of no further value to society, the new competitive mindset seeing no reason to look after a group that could not look after itself. The poor, bereft of their old socialist phrases, now only had the language of

5 Michael Douglas played the rather offensive anti-hero who proclaimed that 'greed, in all its forms: greed for life, for money, for love, knowledge, has marked the upward surge of mankind!'

the market place with which to interpret what had happened to them or to talk through what they should do about it. So when in 2011 a young man named Mark Duggan was shot by police on the streets of Tottenham, London, rather than issuing a clear demand for proper justice and investigation, all the young protesters could think to do was smash shop windows and grab the consumer goods that the new philosophy had taught them to value.

The fourth reason why the poor have not been able to understand their new predicament or to give voice to their complaint is that the *places* where once they came together to discuss such matters have *all but disappeared.* With the demise of heavy industry men and women no longer worked in the same factory or the same industry, they no longer had similar daily routines or working experiences to share, no union meetings to undergird their sense of pride in their skill, and no longer a union structure through which to bargain for their rights. The working men's clubs foundered, and the pubs closed, so even beer drinking became a privatized home-based pursuit rather than a chance to exchange stories and build community. Both women and men found their worlds turned upside-down. The dynamic of home life was radically changed by the presence of the unemployed man, and the women's income, if there was one, became in many cases the staple of the family. Women, who often had only part-time work, were obliged to work full-time, no longer staying at home to do the child-rearing or to support other families. What's more, the stronger women who had so often been the network-builders of the community were now absent, which meant that the culture of the estate was bereft of its strongest defenders. No wonder estates lost their cohesion, and their poorest inhabitants were no longer able to engender the sense of solidarity and shared understanding they needed if they were to make the wider society aware of their true plight.

The council housing estates themselves had once been places where the working class could rely on meeting people who shared a common lifestyle and a sense of togetherness, but as new global forces began to move many into poverty, the supportive community cohesion of the better years rapidly began to diminish and signs of fragmentation became evident. The 'Right to Buy' scheme had inadvertently helped to splinter the estate communities by sowing suspicion between renting tenants and the new home owners and later, during the regeneration phase of the 1980s and 1990s, some sections of the estates were refurbished, others gentrified and others left to fester – sowing more resentment and wariness between neighbouring households. Estates were also changing rapidly from being quite uniform communities, as most estates began offering a wide range of tenancies – multi-occupied rented homes vying for space with housing association and council housing units, together with the occasional owner-occupied home, while the very next street might be managed by one single housing association. The mix of ethnicities began to accelerate too, and small hostel communities of those with special needs were also popping up. Some politicians were even heard to voice their pleasure at seeing the splintering of the Old Labour voting strongholds that the estates had been, but with the demise of so many of the old uniform estates, the poor had been deprived of one more way in which they had traditionally built community, security, a sense of identity and common purpose.

When we take all these factors together – the cuts in welfare benefits, the insecurity of poorly paid employment, the increasing costs of staple foodstuffs and fuel, the myths that blame the poor for their own poverty, the removal of a language to voice their situation, the dismantling of working-class institutions, the loneliness of new migrant arrivals and the isolation born of mixed-tenure housing policies – we begin to see just how heavy-laden and marginalized the poorer tenants of our social housing estates have become.

Although it has only been possible to record a few of the many moving and challenging conversations I have been having during these years of estate visiting and to touch upon just some of the pressures they are now experiencing, I hope this has given the reader a flavour of what it is like to be alongside the poor in Britain today. But before we move on to reflect theologically upon all this, we need to understand the historical factors that have led to poor people now struggling as they do. To some this short foray into history may seem an odd diversion, until we remember how much of the Hebrew Scriptures are themselves historical narratives. They are there because they allow us not only to hear what happened to the Hebrew people, but to receive pointers as to why it happened and how that distinctive history formed them into the people who were to receive Jesus into their midst. Likewise, the story of today's poor will allow us access to much deeper understandings of why Jesus points to them as key to the Kingdom of God and tells them they are blessed.

3

The Story Unfolds

I'm always excited when I visit an estate that is new to me. I like to wander, look and listen, chat to older couples waiting with their shopping bags for the bus, applaud the skate-boarders and BMX riders, as they perform so gracefully and with such skill, visit the schools and the clinics, always asking my usual questions and looking for new ones. And I'm always amazed that people make time to engage with me. I wear my dog-collar, so that they have some idea of where I'm coming from, and now that I'm a pensioner, I clearly don't look as if I pose a threat to anyone. I'm not police, and I'm not a social worker, so they don't assume that I'm spying, and most are pleased to learn that I'm simply interested in their lives and hold them in high regard. They tell me all sorts of things that I suspect other enquirers might not be told. I have a great time!

In this way, by listening carefully to the stories the people themselves share, and looking carefully at the physical realities that assail the senses, I begin to build a picture of life on this or that particular estate and hopefully acquire a sensitivity to its special feel, mood and atmosphere. But as I've done this, it has become clear to me that as well as having its distinctive story to tell, each estate has also been deeply affected and indeed directly shaped by a larger story – the overall history of social housing in Britain from its earliest conception. So I invite the reader to journey with me now as we look briefly at this story and learn together that it has more to teach us about the poor and why they might be blessed than perhaps we were anticipating.

The early housing estates

The idea of large tracts of housing development for multiple occupation goes back to antiquity, even to ancient Rome, where ten- or eleven-storied apartment blocks, or *insulae*, provided accommodation for the poor some 200 stairs up on the topmost floors, while the wealthy lived near to ground level (Aldrete 2004, pp. 79f.). Medieval Cairo boasted seven-storied buildings housing hundreds of the poor, as did Edinburgh's granite tenements of the fifteenth century. We've already made mention of the estates built by the early industrialists of England in the eighteenth century, but it was when government began to play its part that there emerged what we now call 'social housing'. We use the term 'social housing', by the way, to indicate homes that are rented out by non-profit organizations including government itself, and it can be seen today around the world. Nearly half of Hong Kong's current population lives in low-priced council housing. Germany, during the inter-war period of the Weimar Republic, built many estates or *Siedlungen* in Berlin, Cologne and Frankfurt, while France has a very long history of state intervention in housing. But here in Britain social housing has had an extraordinary impact on our history, landscape and upon our social heritage.

The first council estate in the world was built and managed by the London County Council on the boundary of Bethnal Green and Shoreditch in the East End of London. It is still there today, and the visitor can see the wonderful influence of the Arts and Crafts Movement upon its architecture. The 23 blocks of the 'Boundary Estate' radiate out from a central circus of tenements where the notorious slums of the Old Nichol Street Rookery once stood. It is interesting for us to note that these filthy slums had been removed only after a campaign initiated by the Reverend Osborne Jay of Holy Trinity, who had arrived in the parish in 1886 – so the first council housing began from a Christian initiative of care for the poor! Another pioneer was Ebenezer Howard (1850–1928), who thought to take the working class out of the dirty city altogether into new Garden Cities, and in the early years of the new century, the architect and planner Raymond Unwin laid out the Letchworth Garden City in Hertfordshire upon Quaker-owned land to realize Howard's dream that the best of the rural and urban could be united for the benefit of the working classes. However, while these initiatives were extremely praiseworthy, in both these developments, it was evident that only the more 'deserving poor' were allowed to become tenants, since the new rents were set at three shillings a week – an outlay that was beyond the reach of most poor people. The powerful myth of a distinction between the deserving and the undeserving poor had been deeply ingrained in the British psyche for generations, clearly evidenced even in the Elizabethan Poor Laws, and it continues even to this day (Charlesworth and Williams 2014).

Soon after the outbreak of World War One, Prime Minister Lloyd George recognized that the poor had been so badly housed that resultant ill-health had precluded large numbers of men from military service. Additionally, poor men returning from the Front were in a revolutionary mood, as my grandmother was always keen to inform me, and therefore the government pacified them with promises of 'homes fit for heroes'. The Parliamentary Secretary to the Local Government Board writing at the time suggested that, 'the money we are going to spend on housing is an insurance against Bolshevism and Revolution' (Rodger 1992). Then, as so often since, it has appeared to be the case that the poor have only been attended to when they have threatened to become a danger to the established order. The promised council homes were nevertheless to be of a high quality in accordance with the Tudor Walter Standards. These had been steered through Parliament by Dr Christopher Addison, who was later to become the first Health Minister to include housing among his responsibilities. He continued to champion quality housing for the working classes throughout his life, earning him the accolade of 'the father of the council house'. But despite his best efforts, by the outbreak of World War Two, only just over 1,000,000 council dwellings had been built, while middle-class suburban owner-occupation had significantly expanded.

Estates and the rise of the welfare state

The situation at the end of World War Two left the country devastated and vast reaches of workers' housing had been reduced to rubble by the incessant air-raid bombing. But the wartime coalition government had published in 1942 what was to prove a road-map for the future. The Beveridge Report, named after its chairman the economist William Beveridge, identified the existence of five Giant Evils in society: squalor, ignorance, want, idleness and disease, and went on to propose widespread reform, which formed the basis for the post-war social settlement that came to be known as the welfare state. It proposed the expansion of National Insurance, the creation of the National Health Service and, especially important to our study, the huge expansion of council house provision. So when the Labour Party surprised the nation by winning the post-war general election, Aneurin 'Nye' Bevan, the new Minister of Health, spearheaded an onslaught on the housing problem. In the government in 1946 he announced: 'We propose to lay the main emphasis of our programme upon building houses to let. That means that we shall ask local authorities to be the main instruments for the building programme.' They were encouraged to build mixed communities, Bevan proclaiming that, 'segregation of the different income groups is a wholly evil thing. It is a monstrous infliction upon the essential psychological and biological one-ness of the community.' To this end, in addition to replacing housing in the areas flattened by bombing, the government proposed building whole new towns which would be self-contained communities of between 30,000 and 50,000 residents from across the social range, with sufficient jobs for their entire population and all the necessary educational, welfare, health, transport and social facilities needed. The Abercrombie plan of 1944 looked particularly at where these new towns would be situated around London, while similar programmes were mapped out for other parts of the British Isles. The first New Town, Stevenage, was designated in 1947 after fierce local opposition, and in the following year Lewis Silkin, the new Minister of Town and Country Planning, informed a packed public meeting at Laindon School in Essex that 'Basildon will become a City which people from all over the world will want to visit. It will be a place where all classes of community can meet freely together on equal terms and enjoy common cultural recreational facilities' (Wood 2008). By 1950, 13 of these inclusive New Towns had been designated for development. It was a time of hope and promise, as large council housing estates began to take shape. The sense of excitement among the new tenants was palpable, and street parties and public functions added to the feeling that a New Jerusalem was being ushered in.

New Towns did struggle, however, to achieve the diversity of population that Nye Bevan had expected. Basildon, for example, attracted a huge preponderance of skilled manual workers ready to serve the industry that had relocated to local industrial sites, but few unskilled workers and few people in managerial or professional occupations were interested in settling there. All sorts of inducements were offered by government, including a variety of tenure arrangements, but then – as now – the population steadfastly refused to integrate. The dream that council housing would be a means by which the levelling of British society could occur was never to be realized.

Quantity or quality?

In 1945, overall council house completions had already numbered 3,364, but within five years, once they got into their stride, the Labour government had built a million new homes! Not only this, but Nye Bevan was determined that the quality of housing was to be kept high despite the post-war difficulty in obtaining the necessary raw materials. He boasted that 'we shall be judged for a year or two by the number of houses we build. We shall be judged in ten years' time by the type of houses we build.' To showcase the post-war advances, as part of the great 1951 Festival of Britain, the Landsbury Estate was opened in Poplar, East London. Sid Langley, our churchwarden at All Saints Poplar, was keen to tell me how, as one of the first tenants, they'd been proud to show visitors not only the well-constructed houses but the cheap but fine furniture that had been produced to equip them. Throughout this period the average three-bedroomed council house was 37 per cent larger in area than the pre-war equivalent, and houses from this period continue to be highly prized even now.

Nye Bevan in the Commons and Christopher Addison in the Lords worked hard together to maintain these standards, but the Conservative opposition were now realizing how important to the electorate the provision of homes was proving to be, and so the two parties entered into the 1951 election with all guns blazing on the issue. Already Bevan had realized that if he were to maintain standards, he would need to create some breathing space for himself. To this end the government began to turn over the now empty aircraft factories to the manufacture of prefabricated bungalows for the poor. Each 'prefab' had a garden of its own, built-in cupboards and modern conveniences. I remember that in my youth I attended many a cockney party at Mrs B's prefab in the old Woolwich dock lands, where large estates of prefabs were constructed – and continued to be sought after for many years thereafter. But as Bevan built his prefabs, the Conservative Harold Macmillan was heralding in his 'Great Housing Crusade' with a promise that, if elected, a Conservative government would build not merely temporary accommodation but as many as 300,000 new permanent homes a year. In order to do this, he would utilize the more modern and readily available raw materials, aluminium, glass and concrete. Macmillan recognized that to fulfil the dream of a proper home for everyone, he would have to reduce size and building standards to suit, so his new People's House offered an overall reduction in council home size of 13 per cent, while building subsidies were offered to developers to build higher and higher blocks of flats. Over against Bevan's dream that council housing would be the preferred choice of all, Macmillan saw council house tenancy as the poor person's stepping stone to private home-ownership. It was a very different model. He was espousing a new market philosophy and, as the first 'Minister of Housing', he announced in 1954, 'local authorities alone can clear and rehouse the slums, while the general housing need can be met, as it was to a great extent before the war, by private enterprise'.[1] The lower-quality buildings that now replaced the old slums were not always as welcome as Bevan's quality terraces had been, and Poplar's Sid Langley was fond of saying that 'our area had been the prime target of Hitler's Luftwaffe during the war, but they didn't do half the damage to us as Macmillan did with his so-called slum clearances!' On the other hand, for those who had never expected a home of their own, even these smaller units were a cause for rejoicing.

This was the period of the high-rise blocks, erected using so-called 'system-building' techniques, which consisted of clipping together huge precast concrete sections around a central steel framework. It was an unproved method, which unfortunately was soon found to be suffering from bad design, substandard manufacture and poor on-site construction, resulting in such catastrophes as the 1968 disaster at the high-rise Ronan Point where five people died when the side of the block collapsed. But innovation and contemporary modernism had now caught the imagination of the age, and so the 1960s saw the developers and the experimental architects having a heyday, egged on by the government's subsidies. All across the country great towers appeared modelled on the architectural styles of Le Corbusier and Brutalism. But the irony was not lost on the local cockneys when one of these appalling brutalist tenements in my own East London parish was named 'Robin Hood Gardens'. Sheffield's Park Hill Estate and Poplar's Balfron Tower have lately been completely remodelled and gentrified for more wealthy inhabitants, but at the time those who had to live in them preferred to call them 'San Quentin' and 'Stalag 13'. Eventually the establishment came to realize that their grand gestures had not issued in the New Jerusalem they hoped they had been offering. Things became so bad that in February 1974 John Poulson, who had been running a vast architectural practice, was convicted of fraud, while T. Dan Smith, who had had such an impact on the shape of his city that they called him

1 Speech to Urban District Councils Association, June 1954.

'Mr Newcastle', served a six-year prison term for corruption (Grindrod 2013). The poor received no compensation.

In a single year, 1968, the use of these now discredited system-building methods had enabled the construction of no fewer than 450,000 housing units, but the Conservative government had by now decided to divert future funding away from the unpopular high-rise developments towards the refurbishment of older inner-city terraces. Soon the Labour Party were returned to power again largely on a continuing house-building ticket, but by the mid-1970s house-building and maintenance costs were also spiralling out of their control just as another oil-price crisis forced them to re-budget. In 1977 it was necessary for the Party to throw in the towel and announce that from then on they too were regarding Britain as a home-owning nation in accordance with market principles. Significantly, their new housing policy document offered next to no policies regarding council housing and the continuing building of the New Towns shuddered to a halt. The power of international finance had perhaps for the first time had its devastating impact on the housing of Britain's poor.

Council housing had been introduced with laudable acclaim and widely developed as an intended blessing for the poor, and many poor people – like Dotty in our previous chapter – had rejoiced at leaving their damp tenements and unscrupulous landlords for what was for them the New Jerusalem. But the dream had been so often abused by unprincipled developers and well-intentioned but misguided politicians that it left poorer tenants extremely vulnerable to the next turn of history.

'All Change' and the 'Right to Buy': 1979

The year 1979 proved to be a landmark year in the story of housing estates in Britain for by that year as much as 42 per cent of the population lived in council house accommodation. Housing demand, so critical at the end of the war, had at last been met by supply, and local authorities had such an abundance of properties that it was even possible to require them to house anybody found to be homeless. But the standard of the council housing had slipped considerably over the years due to poor construction or lack of maintenance. Some tenants wanted to move to accommodation that suited their larger families, and others would have preferred to be rehoused in areas that did not attract unhelpful neighbours, but on the whole council housing continued to offer a welcomed lifestyle for most tenants. This popularity was evident when Margaret Thatcher swept to power in 1979 and offered tenants the 'Right to Buy' their council homes – an offer that met with tremendous approval by many who immediately invested their savings in the homes they loved. For those who had been tenants for 20 years or more, their home was offered to them at only half the market value with 100 per cent mortgages to assist the purchase. Within two years, 200,000 homes had been sold, but in order to return the overall housing stock to private ownership the legislation made it clear that the money local authorities raised from these sales could not be reinvested in social housing. At the same time, the government forced council rents up for those who had not purchased, so making home-ownership an even more attractive option for those who could afford it. At the beginning of the Thatcher era, council rents in England were 6.9 per cent of average earnings, but by 2002 the percentage had nearly doubled (Jones and Murie 2006, p. 78). In Scotland too, council rents rocketed, squeezing the poor in every housing estate across Britain.

The 'Right to Buy' scheme was just one element within a general government policy of privatization and the redirection of its attention towards the benefits of the new phenomenon of globalization. Globalization came about as a result of three interrelating factors: the introduction of new communication and information technologies, the deregulation of the economic power of the market, and the political determination of Western governments to minimize political and social constraints upon both the economic and technological engines of change. All this resulted in what I have called elsewhere the 'turbo-capitalism' of neo-liberalism (Green 2003, pp. 51–8). The result was that extravagant amounts of excited money fed into a frenzy of spending, short-term investment and fast profits while, in the sphere of industrial manufacture, industrial investment went to those companies that, by utilizing the labour of the poorest of the poor, could manufacture consumer products at knock-down prices. To reap its share of this new available capital Britain required the deregulation of its own financial markets and the depletion within five years of no less than one-third of its manufacturing base, a figure far outstripping all other Western economies. While attention was focused on new office development, the old industrial centres became ghost towns, docks were deserted, mine-shafts filled in, and a landscape of devastation overwhelmed areas that had only recently been bustling with life and manual employment. Skilled workers like Reece in Newcastle, who were especially skilled for the old heavy industries, were now stacking shelves, cleaning offices or acting as security personnel.

The new government quickly realized that it would also be necessary to remove the workers' unions, which they saw as an obstacle to their philosophy of individualism and their policy of stripping out heavy industry. Margaret Thatcher, the Prime Minister, led the battle to remove first the steel workers' union, then the print and then the miners' unions, but in so doing she also silenced any collective voice that poorer people might have had regarding their pay and employment rights. In order to compete in the global market, our workforce was introduced to part-time working, lower wages, zero hours contracts and the expectation of 24/7 availability, while the very poor were squeezed further and further out of the picture altogether.

In the landmark year 1979, there had been more equality of net incomes in the UK than in any other period of its history, but in order to incentivize entrepreneurs increasingly regressive taxation was now introduced. Then in 1981 Michael Heseltine, by then Secretary of State for the Environment, handed over for redevelopment 6,000 acres of the now redundant land in the dock-side area of East London to a new quango – the London Docklands Development Corporation (LDDC). The new body immediately abandoned the Local Authority's plans for social housing and new industry and pushed through their own visionary plan to attract global capital to build a vast development of offices and a finance centre to rival the City of London itself. Through their first five years, the Board's meetings were held in secret, raising legitimate fears that the new developments might bypass the deep-seated problems of the local people. As the local rector during the early years of the building of the new financial centre, I personally witnessed the poor being ignored, alienated and treated as an unwanted irritant. They were doomed to live for years in the midst of dust, noise and disruption, while they watched the area that had once given them security and employment transformed into something that felt to them quite alien. The redevelopment was to be a great success in terms of its awe-inspiring visual impact and it has proved to be a global attraction for London as a financial and commercial city, but it remains very doubtful that it has served the poor who used to live there. For if we take all these initiatives together, we find they have created a situation of intense inequality, which means that now the bottom 50 per cent of the population own only 6 per cent of Britain's wealth, while a top executive can now earn in three days what the average worker will earn in a whole year.

On the other hand, there was so much global finance looking for a home that funds were also injected into Britain's estates, which by 1980 were in dire need of this attention. As we have noted, by the end of the 1970s local authorities had already completely over-extended themselves financially and were no longer able to sustain the cost of maintaining their housing stocks, and incidentally were becoming renowned for their very patronizing attitude towards their tenants. Mac told me:

> You could see the rising damp creeping up the walls, and I proofed it, re-papered and tried everything – I'm a qualified builder after all. I told the Council, because it was clear the building needed proper attention. They had the cheek to tell me it was only condensation, and I should always keep the windows open. They treated me like a spoilt child, but it was my own kids who were getting ill because of it!

Added to these deplorable management failings through the years, there was now the alarming realization that many estates were on the brink of serious social breakdown. In 1985 trouble erupted on the notorious Tottenham housing estate known as Broadwater Farm. It had been built on a wet marshy area liable to flood and housed 1,500 people in 12 system-built tower blocks. Sky-high walk-ways linked the dwellings in a most inhuman style, and, since the estate was not easy to let, the local authority had through the years used it to house their most disruptive tenants alongside many lone parents, the elderly and the abjectly poor. The unemployment rate was running at 42 per cent, and there were 850 burglaries in just one year alone. The new money was therefore directed at the estate but just as things were beginning to improve, in October 1985 the police raided a house looking for a young Jamaican man who was suspected of driving a car without displaying a tax disc. In the tussle that ensued, his mother Cynthia Jarrett was killed by the police. The next night the community vented its anger at the heavy-handedness of local policing, there was disruption on the streets, and PC Keith Blakelock was murdered. These terrible events focused for the whole nation the fact that some of our social housing estates had become very unsafe and unsavoury places. And for the poor the incident signalled how powerless and insignificant they had become – PC Keith Blakelock's name became headline news, while their own Cynthia Jarrett was rarely mentioned.

It was clear that the situation of the poor was once again proving to be a threat to the wider society, and so successive governments thereafter initiated policies intended to turn the poorer housing estates around. With the backing of the now readily available funding, these initiatives took largely three forms: first, the decentralization and improvement of estate housing management, second, increasing residents' involvement in management and other estate activities, and third, substantial periodic investment by local and central government in the estates' infrastructure and property.

New Deals and new structures

In 1997, New Labour swept to power and immediately began to inaugurate a welter of New Deals for the poor. They produced programmes and reports, including the first Urban White Paper (Government 2000) since 1977. It promised to 'deliver an Urban Renaissance', at last viewing the urban no longer as a problem to be solved but as an opportunity to be grasped. Also, at the suggestion of our own National Estates Churches Network, it included the proposal that social housing estates should once again feature in all British urban policy[2] – an inclusion that has continued to this day. Additionally, the government set up a new Social Exclusion Unit, which included church representation, tasked to address the long-term issues of poverty and deprivation. Now at last we believed we had the promise that the concerns and predicament of the poor were firmly on the agenda of modern government in a positive way.

But by now New Labour no longer trusted even their own local authorities to manage the estates well and set about wresting from their control what council housing remained in their hands. Much had already moved into private ownership under the 'Right to Buy' provisions, but in addition they now set about a grand scheme of Stock Transfer, persuading tenants to have their homes transferred from council control across to that of Registered Social Landlords (RSLs) – those not-for-profit organizations such as housing associations which were properly registered as providers of low-cost social housing. Unlike the local authorities, they were allowed to use rental income and additional private finance to maintain their housing stock or to help build new homes. The stock transfer policy was widely taken up and by 2007 over a million former council houses had been transferred to RSLs. The property on the Vange Estate in Basildon was in such need of attention that the tenants gladly voted for transfer, and David

2 The letter of 29 April 1998 to the Cabinet Office was published in Laurie Green, 2000, *The Challenge of the Estates: Strategies and Theology for Housing Estate Ministry*, Urban Bishops' Panel and NECN Press.

Eaton, the vicar, was drafted in to chair the local management team, since he had a business and accountancy background. The tenants were asked how they wanted their homes to be cared for, and enough staff were enlisted by the Registered Social Landlord to make sure that many of the old running sores of poor maintenance and bad management were attended to.

The Social Exclusion Unit, the new body set up to address the issue of poverty, set about its task with enthusiasm and sparked a public debate that raised the public's consciousness of the inseparable link between poverty and social exclusion. It became clear that if the needs of the poor were to be addressed, in addition to the one-off injections of cash into the poorer housing estates it would also be necessary to 'bend' the central government budgets, so that the fundamental causes of inequality at the heart of society might be rectified. But two major problems arose. First, there remained the built-in presumption in the Unit's reports that the way to deal with exclusion was by addressing the excluded rather than the excluders – the symptoms rather than the cause. Second, a programme that was supposed to address the fundamental causes of poverty and exclusion was bound to call for long-term measures, but with the next election looming the Labour government decided to divert funds into projects that would offer short-term gains which the electorate could immediately see, applaud and vote for. The Social Exclusion Unit therefore began to flounder.

Meanwhile, while schemes such as the New Deal for Communities, Neighbourhood Renewal, Sure Start and various Action Zones all began to make an impact, new money continued to pour into the estates through the new Registered Social Landlords. Tenants looked on in amazement as their estates were visited by wealthy financiers, developers, consultants and management organizations. Money was there to pay for demolishing and rebuilding, smartening the environment, 'enveloping' the façades of old properties, and undertaking major refurbishment schemes. But again, the reality for the poor was not as bright as it appeared on the surface. For while many of the estates were buzzing with excitement by day, the more cynical noticed that they were less exciting when the developers returned to their homes each night with a large percentage of the regeneration budget in their own pockets. Social analysts referred to the phenomenon as the 'Leaky Bucket Syndrome', for although millions were being poured into the estates, a very large proportion of that spending leaked away from the estates to those organizations and developers who set up shop there only during the regeneration period and then left once they had capitalized on the readily available development loans.

In 2006, I helped to chair a group of six Christian analysts tasked to look at this extraordinary expansion of housing development, and in our resultant publication *Building Utopia?* (Green and Baker 2008) we alerted readers to the vulnerability of the whole enterprise. Soon after, as we now know to the nation's cost, the whole economic bubble proved unsustainable and, as debts were called in, global confidence collapsed, issuing in the international financial catastrophe of 2008. Finance was withdrawn, building sites closed, mortgages foreclosed, and New Labour was driven from power. Funding for new initiatives was withdrawn, localized management and enhanced maintenance proved unsustainable, unemployment bit hard, and once again the future began to look bleak. And while all were affected, it was the poor who, as ever, suffered most from the cut-backs.

The Cameron years

In 2010 the Conservative and Liberal Democrat parties agreed to work together to form a new Coalition government under the Premiership of David Cameron. It blamed the preceding Labour government for leading the country into a debt-driven financial disaster and promised a policy of even more austere cuts in government expenditure in order to return the country to growth and stability, with many of those cuts mainly impacting the poor.

The other main plank of the Coalition government's manifesto was its promise to address the dearth of affordable housing. It was salutary to note for example that in London's Tower Hamlets, where the nation's highest incidence of child poverty was to be found, gentrification had made it necessary to have an income of at least £75,000 a year to buy a local home! The government therefore announced a target of 335,000 new affordable homes to be built by 2018 and gave the task of providing them to the social housing sector. On the BBC *File on Four* programme (Sunday, 22 October 2013) David Ore of the National Housing Federation said that he had applauded the announcement until the government's own 2010 Comprehensive Spending Review cut the promised funding for these new homes by no less than one-third, the biggest percentage cut of any sector of the budget. This meant that housing associations were being told to make bricks without straw, because they were left with only two equally unpalatable funding sources. The first was through increasing rents on their properties, which had the effect of trapping poorer tenants further into housing benefit dependency. The second was by negotiating very large loans to build very expensive properties which they could then sell to generate profit with which to build the affordable homes. However, a number of associations on entering into these complex financial deals then realized that they were totally out of their depth in a world of high finance that they did not fully understand. It was an even greater shock for the housing associations' tenants to learn that their own rented homes had been offered as security against the massive loans, so the poor stood to lose everything if the deal backfired, which of course it sometimes did. So with the social housing sector unable to find the funds to meet the government's targets for building affordable homes, and the promise of yet further cuts, it will again be the poor who stand to suffer most.

So have the poor been blessed?

We have only had space to touch briefly upon some highlights of the history of British social housing, but on our way we have recognized a number of the early champions of the poor like Nye Bevan, Christopher Addison and the Revd Osborne Jay, who prepared the ground for the first council housing. Additionally we have commended the initiatives of successive governments in attempting to address the needs of the poor, especially for affordable and adequate housing. It is salutary therefore to look back and evaluate the outcomes of the many well-intentioned policies. In 2006 Rebecca Tunstall and Alice Coulter produced a very carefully researched report, *Twenty-five Years on Twenty Estates* (Tunstall and Coulter 2006), in which they sought to evaluate the effects on estates of all government improvement initiatives over the 25 preceding years. On the whole, the researchers were very impressed by the policies and reported: 'These formerly very unpopular estates have become more "normal" as majority social housing areas, in terms of popularity, the mix of tenure and landlords, the level of management decentralization, and management performance.' However, they went on to make two rather startling observations.

First, they noted that 'some of the changes in population may be due to disadvantaged people leaving these estates, and both mixed tenure and increased popularity may also make it more difficult for the most disadvantaged to gain homes in the improved areas' (p. xiii). So the report acknowledges that while it is possible to claim that the geographical areas themselves had been improved, the result was that the poor had been priced out altogether and forced away into the very cheap and even worse estates. Second, the researchers believed that 'improvements achieved in these estates are unlikely to be sustainable without ongoing support [such as] strong housing and labour markets, which may not continue. One senior manager said: "The market is changing faster than ever before . . . it could change in another way in the future"' (p. xiii). He was proved to be right when only one year after the publication of the report the boom turned to extravagant bust, and even the best estates started to see the devastating effects once more of unemployment, distanced management and withdrawal of support services.

Other research reports[3] have also looked at the consequences of more specific housing policies, not least the 'Right to Buy' legislation, pointing out that while the sale of council houses resulted in the expected rise in home-ownership, it also

3 See, for example, Coles *et al.* 1998; Fitzpatrick and Stephens 2009; Hills 2007; Jones and Murie 2006.

produced a striking reduction of 50 per cent of those rental units available to the needy. 'You used to be able to put in for a transfer', said Jane, 'but now there's so few council houses you sit tight and hang on to the bannisters! It used to be lovely round here, but there's so few council houses left they had to squeeze people in who are really on the bread-line. They haven't got a chance of making the place look nice – decent curtains and all that – so the whole blasted place is going downhill!' Meanwhile many of those who did undertake a 'Right to Buy' purchase have found themselves in debt, unable to finance the 100 per cent mortgages that they contracted when they were still in employment. In 2013, Shelter's Roger Harding reported that, statistically, 'Right to Buy' mortgage holders are far more likely than other purchasers to have their home repossessed due to negative equity. Many repossessed flats and houses have been bought at auction for knock-down prices, and as the years have progressed, many homes originally purchased from the council under the 'Right to Buy' scheme have now fallen into the hands of private landlords who on some estates are clearly charging very high rentals, are overcrowding the accommodation, and are being very lax with repairs and maintenance. The estates have suffered and the poor tenants have lost the security they once cherished.

The earliest housing estates promised so well and many fine people were involved in their story, but as our brief history has demonstrated, there have been factors in operation that have at times turned the promised New Jerusalem into the last place you would ever choose to live. Residence on the poorest social housing estates has through the years become the tenure of last resort. Many estates remain pleasant and spacious, but some have been singled out to become the depositories of those people who seem to mean very little now to our present society. They are residualized and forced to live in very unsavoury conditions in these ghettoes of the poor. Here they experience all the attendant threats of community disintegration, stresses upon family relationships, closure of local facilities and absence of appropriate employment. They are out of sight and out of mind.

Despite all the odds

As we have surveyed this extraordinary history, certain factors have surfaced that are particularly pertinent regarding our concern to understand the condition of the poor, and it is helpful briefly to remind ourselves of these factors before we move on. First, from the earliest times people have been pleased to make a comforting distinction between the deserving and the undeserving poor, and although the facts discredit this distinction, it remains for some a viable excuse to ignore one of the most potent problems of our age – poverty. Second, some have only bothered about the poor when they have appeared a danger to the wider society, while, third, there has been an entrenched refusal to respond to policies that seek to bring the rich and poor together. Sometimes that abiding division runs along class lines while others have promoted a philosophy of individualism and have therefore left the poor to see to their own needs. Often the poor seem to have been used as a political football, although there have been some who have sought to implement programmes and policies based on a strong ethical belief in justice and equal opportunity. Some have deregulated controls on the accumulation of wealth as a matter of principle, believing that the benefits will eventually trickle down to all – a theory that unfortunately never seems to cash out in practice. There has certainly been little careful listening to the poor through the course of this history and most policies have descended upon them from on high, from well-meaning but ill-informed politicians. This top-down approach has issued in outcomes that beg the question, 'Who in fact has most benefited from these policies?' Global factors too have impacted the poor as investment has followed the cheapest labour markets, and the policy of stripping away our own industrial manufacturing base has increased the number of unemployed and offered only feeble employment to many of the population.

Global forces have also produced surplus capital that has been used to regenerate and gentrify the old haunts of the inner-city poor, pricing them out and forcing them to disrupt their lives and move out. Unemployment, the 'Right to Buy' and a general inflation in costs have all played their part in increasing debt for the poor, who are rarely able to repay, and predators of all sorts gather around. Their life becomes ever more precarious and vulnerable, and as they become increasingly dependent, so the bureaucracy set up to be of service to them imposes unjust sanctions and becomes ever more patronizing and complex. The poor bear the brunt of the government's increasing number of austerity policies and are made fun of on TV and in the media – demonized for supposedly being the authors of their own poverty. People are told that the poor are the cause of the country's economic problems and they are squashed together into the most run-down of the remaining social housing. And with the demise of the unions and the move of the major political parties away from addressing their needs, they have no voice with which to gainsay the myths.

Yet this truly grim history has been played out against the backdrop of a remarkable phenomenon. For despite all the ravages of poverty and demonization, those who actually live out their lives on our poorest estates are often good to be with. They still take pride in being local, they retain that heart which will go out of its way to care for others in need, often putting our own caring to shame. Yes, there are many exceptions where the grim circumstances have impressed their disabling mark upon people and left them despairing, angry or apathetic, but where does the resilience come from that has enabled most people to live through this history and still laugh with their friends? There is a resilience here in the face of being sinned against for generations that few ever acknowledge. Professional visitors and first-time buyers on these estates are usually not aware of much of this, because they see the place only as a stepping stone on their own journey and only meet the locals at their most defensive and untrusting. But those who dig deep unearth in the poor a capacity to care that is in sharp contrast to the inadequate policies that have descended upon them from above. There is certainly a blessedness here, even though it is enigmatic and elusive. Unravelling that enigma poses a significant social and theological challenge, so it is fitting that it is to theology that we now turn.

4

Praying the Kingdom Prayer

With the voices of the poor ringing in our ears, reminding us of their hardships and joys, their frustrations and aspirations, together with all that we have learned from our brief history of how our estates came to be the way they are, we come to that part of our theological process where we look at all these experiences and facts from the perspective of our Christian faith. This will allow the lives of the poor to impact upon our understanding of our faith, and in turn will allow our Christian faith to reflect upon all we have learned from the poor of our estates. We might picture this dynamic as an interplay of revelations: the revelations that come to us through our experiences and the revelations that come to us through the texts, doctrines and stories of our faith. I can call this an interplay of revelations because our experience of being alongside poor people on our estates tells us that God is very present and evident there, while God is also most assuredly there in the stories and revelations of the Christian faith. Our task is now to discern how one revelation speaks to the other, or to use our usual terminology, how each is reflected in the other – hence theological 'reflection'. The key to good theological practice is to listen: to listen with rapt attention to the people and places in which we are set; to listen to the Bible and the other great treasures of faith through which God's heart is opened to us; to listen diligently to the promptings of the Holy Spirit within; to listen to the connections all these things make together; and finally to listen to where that leads us. This is a form of listening that is similar to reflective prayer for it demands our deepest attention. It requires us to make no prior assumptions about outcomes but to analyse critically what we hear, in order to discern the sometimes unexpected activity of God within it all.

In *Let's Do Theology* (Green 2009) I have described some of the many ways of enabling theological reflection to happen, but in this case I would like us to concentrate our attention upon just one central and fundamental Bible text which is known by heart by Christians around the world – the Lord's Prayer – and see what light each phrase of that prayer throws upon all that we have been hearing and learning about the experience of poor people on our estates. I have chosen this particular text largely because it will remind us that prayer should be at the very heart of any theological endeavour. It was Karl Barth, perhaps the greatest Protestant theologian of the twentieth century, who said: 'The first and basic act of theological work is prayer' (1963). Centuries before that, Evagrius of Pontus wrote that 'a theologian is one whose prayers are true'.[1] I believe both these insights to be profoundly valid, and it would seem that Matthew is of the same mind, since he places the Lord's Prayer right at the heart of Jesus' extended theological treatise, the Sermon on the Mount (Matt. 6.9–13), making prayer both structurally and theologically the pivot of that Sermon. One scholar says that by placing it thus, Matthew 'dissolves the line between theology and worship' (Boring 1995), since both theology and prayer are supremely creative ways of bringing together our faith and our daily lives. Sometimes the impression is given that prayer and theological reflection are very calming and serene activities but, on the contrary, the task of putting ourselves before God with the situations of human life on our hearts can be a very disturbing experience, akin to the struggle of Jacob where, according to Genesis 32.23–32, he wrestles with an angel by the Brook of Jabbok. Prayer and theology can be, as they were for Jacob, a strenuous tussle with God's truths and sometimes, again like Jacob, we only receive the blessing of them when we come limping away – for I have to admit that the outcome of this book may prove just too uncomfortable for some.

1 See Green 2009, p. 14.

It was as early as about AD 205 when Tertullian, the Roman commentator, wrote the first known essay on the Lord's Prayer and towards the beginning of that work he referred to the Prayer as 'a summary of the Gospel' (Tertullian 1993, p. 681), and scholars through the centuries have stood by his assertion. As my dear friend Bishop Kenneth Stevenson put it, 'The description fits, because in the Lord's Prayer we find a rare penetration of all that Jesus taught and stood for and did' (Stevenson 2000, p. 41). It is the most ecumenical and yet radical prayer imaginable, to which nearly all people of goodwill can ascribe. We always do well to remember of course that careful New Testament scholarship has helped us realize how overlaid with interpretive editing some of the evangelists' records of the sayings of Jesus are. We therefore always have to bear that in mind in our reading of the Gospels. But in this case scholars tell us that there is no need to doubt that the Lord's Prayer is almost in every regard the authentic invention of Jesus himself – even its nearest contemporary parallel, the traditional Hebrew *Kaddish* Prayer, being significantly different. We can with confidence therefore look to the Lord's Prayer to discern the key elements of the Christian gospel and use that as a template against which to reflect upon what the poor have been telling us.

Although the Lord's Prayer must be understood as a dynamically interrelated whole, we can nevertheless, for these purposes at least, dare to meditate on each phrase in turn, allowing a free flow of connections to arise in our minds with the stories and facts we have been exploring.

Our *Father*: God's intimate concern

Both Matthew and Luke record the words of the Lord's Prayer for us, although in slightly differing versions. Matthew offers us a somewhat longer version, probably derived from the particular worshipping community to which he belonged. It might also be that Jesus himself offered slightly different versions of the prayer from time to time, when he was first teaching his disciples. But the sentiments of both versions are very much the same – and both begin by addressing God as Father. Many poorer estate tenants find it hard at first to think about God as Father, because their experiences of human fatherhood may have been very negative. Indced, their relationships with any authority figures may have been very far from pleasant. But the scholars help us here by showing how the biblical text of the Prayer is clearly derived from an Aramaic original – Jesus taught the Prayer in the common language of the people, not the Greek into which it was later translated. And the Aramaic word for 'father', which he used here, is 'Abba' – 'Daddy'! Abba was the word a child would have used of a loving parent, although it was also used by adults to address their father in a very intimate and loving way, so it would not have sounded silly for Jesus to have told his adult followers to use the word. It certainly worked for Michael, a new Christian from a Northern Ireland estate:

> What I like about church is that they talk about God the father who actually loves you! Imagine that! My father left us before I ever got started! But God gets you back on track, see. Now I know there's a chance for me with my partner. I can try and be more like that, see, and be there for my kids.

The theologian Joachim Jeremias was convinced that Jesus was the first to call God 'Abba', although this is now sometimes disputed (D'Angelo 1992), but clearly this usage was so distinctive of Jesus that it became lodged in the hearts of Christians as fundamental to the Prayer and our understanding of how God wants us to relate to him. What Jesus did therefore was to turn a doctrine about the fatherhood of God into an intimate and intense experience of relationship. He knew God to be his own loving father and invited his followers to share in that intimacy (John 17.21). Inspired by this new insight, other great authorities such as Anselm of Canterbury and Mother Julian of Norwich went on to speak of God as mother, standing alongside the father image to help us appreciate just how warm and loving our relationship with God can be. Indeed, to emphasize the point Jesus also used feminine imagery of himself as a mother hen caring for her chicks

(Matt. 23.37) and always spoke of the Holy Spirit as feminine as was the Hebrew tradition. I think we should too.

Parenthood is generally very highly esteemed by the poor, but on the poor estates I have been constantly in the company of parents who are extremely distressed about not being able to provide properly for their children. They are usually accepting of having to go without themselves, but lose sleep for fear that their children will go hungry or lose their home. Samantha was adamant: 'I don't give a damn about me, it's my kids that are important to me. It makes me feel like a bit of sh*t to stand in this queue lining up for a handout, but if I have to I will, as long as my Paul and Robbie don't go without.' Many parents among the poor appear outwardly to be quite selfish, but the closer we look, the more we realize the reality is usually very different. Some women, always the bearers of the most exacting aspects of poverty, even bear severe beatings in order to protect their children and to make sure they are provided for. And just as any caring parent is expected to provide for their children, so the poor expect society to do the same by caring for its weakest members, especially in the provision of proper shelter – as is recognized in Article 25 of the Universal Declaration of Human Rights. But it happens that I am writing this chapter in the middle of a very cold night while on duty at our local night shelter for the homeless, surrounded by poor brothers and sisters for whom even that most basic right has been denied.

The Lord's Prayer opens with words that assume that God the Father wants to see all God's children properly provided for, feel secure to grow, and know that the authorities are on their side. Our historical survey has shown, however, that subsequent to Bevan's vision of council homes for all, the state's role in housing provision was thereafter reduced to a 'safety net' function – caring only for those who had fallen on hard times. And more recently its role has changed again to an 'ambulance function' – there to help for only a very short period those who are in dire need. Indeed, society now seems less committed to seeing houses as homes for its citizens and more concerned to see housing as a financial investment for those who have the money. It is little wonder that many on very poor housing estates experience those in authority not as a caring parent but as aloof and uninterested, while the Lord's Prayer points us to a God whose Kingdom relates intimately to all its citizens under a loving Father who wants to see all his children well-provided for.

Our Father: belonging together

Both versions of the Lord's Prayer are clearly expressed in the plural form, so although Luke begins simply by addressing God as 'Father', Matthew is right to add the obvious addition – *Our* Father. All having one father implies, of course, that we belong together in one family, and also that we are in a familial relationship with Jesus, the Son of the Father. John makes that very clear when Jesus prays 'may they all be one, just as, Father, you are in me and I am in you, so that they also may be in us' (John 17.21). So in our Kingdom life together we must rejoice in affirming our togetherness as brothers and sisters one with another and with Jesus himself, and make every opportunity to discover what we have in common, and celebrate our solidarity as one family. We'll remember that Nye Bevan saw it as a moral imperative that all classes should be housed in close proximity in order to express this common humanity, and recent governments have continued to espouse this principle by requiring developers to provide a mixture of housing wherever possible. Developers have often responded, however, by appending new estates to old only to separate them off by constructing a busy road or even a boundary wall, and by giving the new areas names that are distinctly different from the original estate, so that they will be more marketable to new buyers. Even when estates are newly built as mixed-tenure housing, it is not long before the community itself divides into sub-communities of more like-minded people. A friend tells me that having bought into such an estate he soon learned by experience to avoid those neighbours who parked expensive cars on their forecourt, and instead formed friendships with those whose cars were similar to his own. To an outsider or planner the estate looked mixed, but the residents were actually inhabiting parallel universes. Perhaps this is why the rich don't understand the poor or the poor the rich, because they never really meet. The vicar of an estate in Brentwood tells me that it boasts a very fine primary school, but those who consider themselves 'aspiring' have chosen to send their children to a school outside the estate in order to keep them separated from the poorer children. The irony is that the school to which they are now driving each day does not provide such a fine education as the school on their own estate.

But neither do the poor themselves always see others as brothers and sisters, and some poor estates have become breeding grounds for extreme right-wing sentiments, violence and racism. In Shadwell the white community accuses local Bangladeshis of living cosy lives at their expense, not realizing that often those Asian family members are under such pressure that they have to take sleeping-bag turns to occupy one bed with as many as 14 squashed into a two-bedroom flat. So poor communities are divided from one another in hateful antagonism when in fact they are one in sharing similar experiences.

While the Prayer emphasizes our unity as children of one heavenly Father, society at large often tries to convince us that poor people are a species apart. Some government publications have played their part in promoting disharmony by accusing the poor estates of harbouring: '[a] "culture of worklessness" or "poverty of aspiration" . . . generating a vicious and self-perpetuating cycle leading not only to high levels of worklessness but also to crime, deprivation and social exclusion' (Government 2003, p. 50). Comments like this make George very angry:

> They call us lazy 'cos we won't take lousy jobs. I'd take any job, do anything, but only if there was some security with it. Most offer terrible wages and don't last longer than a few months. Then you're out on your ear again through no fault of your own, and this time your benefits have been stopped 'cos you've had a job. And you don't get those benefits back for months after the job finishes. How are you expected to feed your family then? Give us the chance of a steady job – even emptying bins will do – and we'd jump at it!

So the problem remains, how might it be possible to bring people together so that one group is not intimidated, dominated or patronized by another, but all recognize how much we share in common? If that could be achieved, our differences could become our treasures and no longer causes of disharmony and distrust. But trust cannot be realized without there being at least a degree of justice between the various groups in our society, and this is a tough call when more than half the households of those still looking for work are living on a total income of less than £6,000 a year (Fitzpatrick and Stephens 2009, p. 146). The Church must itself accept and teach the wider society that the Lord's Prayer really does expect us to acknowledge that we are all children of our one heavenly Father, and that it cannot be right to treat our family members in this way.

Our Father *in heaven*: acknowledging the beauty

The words 'in heaven' remind us of God's transcendence and otherness and raise our sights to a realm of sublime beauty and serenity. But on so many of our estates there is only drab concrete and brutalist architecture, badly maintained walk-ways, boarded-up shopping precincts and churches that look abandoned. Despite this there is often a sense of togetherness and mutual support, which has a beauty of its own, and a determination and resilience that transcends the pressures which seek to grind people down. It is interesting, for example, to see how the old Church of St Albans on the Becontree Estate is suddenly attracting local people, who on entering the building for the first time find their breath taken away by the soaring heights of the architecture. It's a traditional-looking church, built for the Estate by the Wills tobacco family with the stated intention of bringing something beautiful to a poor community, inspiring and uniting, helping people to worship the God who is within the community and yet so far above it. On the other hand, when Milton Keynes was provided with a modern church at its centre, many local people felt it was too secular in style and instead looked to the old traditional village churches on the periphery of the vast new estate – buildings where they found it easier to sense the otherness of God. Unfortunately, however, that did not help them to recognize the beauty and otherness of God *within* the ordinariness of their estate.

In Exodus 3 we are told that Moses saw a burning bush, and while being aware of the ordinariness of the bush, he also discerned that there was something within it that was clearly of the beyond – so holy that he removed his shoes in the presence of the Other. And while Moses was still reeling in awe and fear, he heard God's passionate concern for the Hebrew people in slavery in Egypt, for this transcendent God was still Abba, the Father who cared for his children. And the Lord's Prayer alerts us to this paradox by calling God our Father *in heaven.* Like Moses, we should stand in awe of the God of heaven – but learn from Jesus that God is also our loving and concerned Father. In the same way, the Disciples have to get used to the fact that Jesus, their friend and brother, is liable at any time to transfigure into the sublime Other (Matt. 17.1–8). And on the estate we have to learn to expect such transcendence in what we thought to be only mundane. Even if we are surrounded by a lacklustre housing estate environment, Kingdom people are called upon to recognize the heavenly presence and realize that even here heaven is not so remote.

A very strange tale is told about heaven in Psalm 82. There we hear God accusing the 'lesser gods' of failing in their duty to 'rescue the weak and the needy, save them from the clutches of the wicked' (v. 4). And God deems this to be such a heinous omission on their part that he takes from the lesser gods their immortality. They must die, no longer worthy of their place in heaven. The psalm makes very clear that heaven demands that justice be shown to the poor and needy and that our heavenly Father sees this as a matter of life and death – no optional extra! The transcendent God who is yet present even in the mundane housing estate brings from the realm of heaven a love that is shot through with justice for the poor.

Hallowed be your Name: what is worth honouring?

'Hallowed be your Name' is a phrase which, if it were not for its familiarity, would sound very strange to a modern ear. What has someone's name got to do with anything, and just what does it mean to hallow something?

In the Middle Eastern mind and today in many other parts of the world too, the name of a person is much more than just a title, but is meant to signify their whole nature and destiny. Time and again in the Bible we see how a name is given to a prophet or a patriarch, for example, to tell us about their inner purpose and character. I have a dear African friend who bears the name 'Gift', and I have always been taken by how that name has encouraged and supported him through his many years of suffering and struggle. So where the Lord's Prayer says that God's name is to be hallowed, we are to understand that God's very nature and person is to be reverenced and held in the highest honour.

Pete Hillman invited me to attend his Essex church as a guest. It is a large warehouse that has within it vast ramps for skate-boarding and BMX riding – and the young members of his congregation use their skills in the urban arts as worship and to reach out in mission.[2] They have become aware just how close God is to them on the streets of the estate, and they touch some of that excitement in their 'homage on wheels', as they give glory to God and 'hallow the Name'.

But as God brings us all into his family as brothers and sisters, each made in our heavenly Father's image, so honouring and hallowing the name of our father implies too that we should honour his image in his children. Estate people often talk about needing a 'bit of respect', and this yearning indicates how withering and dehumanizing it can be not to be honoured for that spark of God that is within each of us as one of his children. 'You know, Father, I'm fed up with people who don't know us from Adam slagging off our estate! What right have they got to keep on about us being deprived and needy all the time? It's not as if they do anything to

2 www.legacyweb.org.

help – it's just that they enjoy having a dig!' When some young women today go to the job centre in search of employment, they see against their name a ticked box which labels them as NEETs, meaning 'not in employment, education or training' – categorized according to what they are not, rather than honouring them for who they are. For a young person their first proper job marks their transition into adult life, affirms them and sets them on their way as an acknowledged contributor to society, but consigning them to a negative self-image at such an age is to besmirch the name of the God who has created them with talent and energy. It takes away their self-respect, their destiny, and consigns them to silence. The young virgin, Mary of Nazareth, when first she realized that God had not left her redundant but given her a great work to do, found her voice and sang her Magnificat song. No longer had she to wait for others to speak for her, but she became the voice of the poor, singing out her radical freedom song: 'My soul magnifies the Lord!' So often the voice of the poor is not heard – they appear only as a statistic on a print-out. But in the Church Mary's name is hallowed as the Bible bids us (Luke 1.48), and she in turn points us to her Lord, that we may above all hallow his name, that at his name every knee should bow (Phil. 2.10).

When the BBC descended upon the Harpurhey Estate in Manchester, they promised to produce a programme that celebrated the vibrancy of the local people, but when broadcast, it portrayed estate residents as depraved and dysfunctional. Mike McGurk, the minister of Christ Church, along with his fellow estate residents, was furious and took to the streets to protest. When the local people saw their parish priest up in arms, they took him to their hearts. One local shopkeeper said Mike had 'told people the good news about the estate' rather than the BBC's distortion of the facts – he had hallowed the name of the Harpurhey Estate and, in so doing, had hallowed the presence of God shining through its people. They no longer had to feel ashamed.

Many poor people are ashamed of their poverty – shame that causes them anger and many tears – prompting them to take out suicidal loans so that their children can have the latest branded goods and so not be bullied in school. But to be affirmed for who they truly are, to be honestly listened to and be called by their name rather than labelled, can heal that shame and let them stand tall once again. Mary Magdalene as she cries in despair in the garden by the empty tomb hears Jesus say her name, 'Mary', and she is changed (John 20.16). During the confirmation service, the bishop lays praying hands upon the head of the new Christian and says: 'God has called you by name and made you his own.' Each one is caught up by the Spirit of God and affirmed by name. In the world it seems at times that we are taught only to value our most avaricious selves – as the L'Oreal advert puts it, 'because you're worth it'. But real worth is not just skin deep, but derives from the fact that God has created us as his beloved children, to honour his name and to recognize and acclaim his beauty and presence in one another even if we live on the most unlikely estate.

Your Kingdom come: a new world order

The Lord's Prayer is often called 'the Kingdom Prayer', and rightly so, for its words point us constantly to the Kingdom or Reign of God, which is mentioned explicitly twice and implied throughout. And just as the Kingdom is central to the Prayer, so it was absolutely central in the ministry and teaching of Jesus. He took hold of this word 'kingdom', with all its malevolent overtones of Rome and the Herods, and subverted it, deconstructed it and redefined it, asserting before Pilate: 'Mine is not a Kingdom of this world!' (John 18.36). In his preaching Jesus proclaimed: 'The time is fulfilled, and the kingdom of God is close at hand. Repent, and believe the gospel' (Mark 1.15). During his itinerant ministry, Jesus 'made his way through towns and villages, preaching and proclaiming the good news of the kingdom of God' (Luke 8.1). He sent out his disciples with the commission, 'as you go, proclaim that the kingdom of Heaven is close at hand' (Matt. 10.7), and he told them that at the final judgement those who have cared for the oppressed will be rewarded – 'take as your heritage the kingdom prepared for you' (Matt. 25.34). He taught his disciples to pray: 'Thy kingdom come', and on his cross was emblazoned the inscription 'The King of the Jews' (Matt. 27.37). At every turn of his ministry and from the cross itself, it is to the Kingdom that Jesus points.

Many people find the word 'kingdom' difficult with all its allusions to authority and male dominance. The poor have very often experienced how power can be badly abused by those in authority, be it in the family, the local housing office or even in the countries from which they have fled as asylum-seekers. At the same time, if the atmosphere on their estate is menacing and chaotic, to pray for a regime or 'kingdom' of trust and harmony can be life-promising. 'We believe that there's going to be something different from all this, don't we?' said Carol. 'Sometimes I get the feeling though that it's never going to come, especially after last night's fight on our corner. But every now and again it feels it's just round the corner. It's a bit like the sunshine I suppose.' Rather than speak of 'kingdom' some have substituted the word 'reign' as an alternative, for at least it gets rid of the male connotations. But whichever we prefer, it is important to remember that Jesus takes hold of a word that, in the light of the Jewish and Roman kingdoms of his time, was even more unpalatable and controversial than it is today and reconstructs it in a most extraordinary way. He deliberately takes this unsavoury word and invests it with new and compelling meaning so as to alert us to its challenging reversal and potency. The poor with whom Jesus lived experienced political, economic, spiritual and social oppression from their Roman overlords and their Jewish leaders, but Jesus demonstrated in his life and death how God's love overturns all their previous understandings of kingship. They see in him glimpses of a new world order.

We see these glimpses today when we experience relationships being healed in the homes and on the streets of poor estates, so often crawling with harshness, isolation and negativity. One Saturday morning, I found an elderly and unkempt woman asleep in our church porch, homeless and alone. I sat there on the step talking with her, trying to offer some comfort, when a member of our congregation on her way back from the market came and sat with us on the step. She simply said to the woman: 'come home and live with us'. She helped her to her feet and, supporting her carefully, took her to her own small home to care for her there. This sort of extreme self-giving is not unusual among the poor, for it derives from a deeper awareness of injustice than most of us can muster. They are more attuned to issues of injustice because they experience them daily and cry out for an alternative 'kingdom': 'This is not fair, Father! Just when we're getting our lives together again they hit us with more cuts! They tell us, go get a job – when I've already got a job and still can't feed my kids! We need a different sort of system altogether.' We hear a yearning for an alternative kingdom, a life-changing and just transformation.

In the midst of this harsh alienation, we find such extraordinary signs of tenants working together for the common good and youngsters determined to be positive, caring for their neighbours and going out of their way to celebrate the good things of life together. All this alerts us to the fact that the Kingdom is even now breaking in upon a tired world. We pray earnestly therefore that the Kingdom will soon come in all its fullness. And this prayer has such an urgency about it, it is so heartfelt and unfeigned that it echoes the prayer that we hear in the New Testament from the very earliest Christians – it even comes to us in their original Aramaic language – *Maranatha* – 'Come, Lord Jesus', establish your Kingdom now! (1 Cor. 16.21.)

Your will be done, on earth as in heaven: living out the Kingdom

We must not lose sight of the urgency of this *Maranatha* prayer, heard even today from our poor estates, albeit in such different language. Those who live comfortable lives are content to think of the Kingdom of God as something in the distant future, in the after-life or even at the end of the world – but the Lord's Prayer soon dispels that notion. It asks that God's will be done here and now, just as surely as it is done in heaven. The prayer does not allow us to do the usual 'churchy' thing and conjure with abstractions, for in the incarnation of Jesus, God quite literally gets 'down to earth' with us, and on the cross we see the determination of Jesus to live this prayer in action, 'on earth as in heaven'. That cross, the Tree of Life, has its roots deep in the darkness of the soil – in every dark alleyway of the estate, in the crack-house and in the despair of the poor – and from that rootedness in our dark reality the Tree takes a mysterious sustenance and bursts into the light above sending out leaves and blossom and new life. And as those leaves and blossoms eventually fall back to the ground they feed the soil which in turn gives strength and sustenance to the roots in their darkness, amid the shuttered shops and broken bus shelters. The blood of the cross, like his mother's blood surrounding his birth, unites Jesus with the realities of our humanity, and it is God's ownership of this, our messiness, that alone transforms it. When I sat with Dotty in the kitchen of her estate flat, she was fully aware of the messiness, indeed the horror of much that was around her, but she was also able to look at the surrounding trees, think of the deeper story they could tell, and befriend the youngsters waiting for the bus. She had told me a simple story, but her love for the estate and for those youngsters – and indeed her radiance – spoke of another dimension within it all. Like her, it is incumbent upon us to sink ourselves in the poor housing estate, so that we too see in the dark places the ever-present Jesus, healing, saving and bringing to glory.

In his incarnation Christ broke for ever the barrier between the secular and the sacred, between God's will on earth and in heaven. The things of earth matter so much to his Kingdom that Jesus became deeply embedded in his own Palestinian culture, taking it very seriously and pointing us to the Kingdom breaking into it. Following his lead we must therefore deepen our commitment to and sharpen our awareness of our earthly setting, our 'here and now', by careful analysis of our context – just as we are seeking to do in this study. This will ensure that we do not allow our theological reflection to issue in abstraction and inaction. This is the praxis of which we spoke earlier. It is the dynamic interplay of action and reflection, committed action and informed reflection, that allows our actions to be shot through with godly meaning and our meanings to issue in intentional actions. This enables us to view the worldly realities through the lens of the heavenly and to glimpse signs of the Kingdom in places that we had not expected to find them. In our estate churches, for example, we see laity and clergy engaging politically together, attending negotiation meetings, setting up public gatherings, confronting the powerful, developing projects and groups to shine as lights in the darkness. Night shelters, foodbanks, breakfast clubs, credit unions, toddlers' clubs, cell groups, lunch clubs, Meals on Wheels, training projects, parenting courses, urban gardens, art groups, prisoner support, alcohol and drug awareness centres – and so the list goes on and on. And the very significant thing about so many of these groups and projects is precisely that they are 'significant' – they signify something much larger than themselves. In themselves they may be quite small and marginal, but each can act out and witness to God's will being done on earth as in heaven. That's why Jesus made sure that his every undertaking – his miracles, his actions and parables – while inevitably particular to that time and place, were each symbolic and sacramental of his universal Kingdom. This means that in our contemporary estate life and ministry we must value every little Kingdom action, because it has the propensity to speak of, and even participate in, something much bigger than it is in itself. It can be a pointer to that which holds the universe together.

Many congregations on our estates are very small indeed and setting up projects and clubs like this may be beyond their capacity. But they too can and do play a similarly 'significant' and sacramental role in their communities. Martin Wharton, as Bishop of Newcastle, was fond of saying: 'small churches are not failed big churches', and he fought hard to draw the Church of England's attention to the profound value of these small sparks of light in dark urban places. The University of Liverpool's Centre for Urban Studies produced a paper in 1989 entitled *The Servant Church in Granby*, which spoke of just such a small congregation as 'representing an enduring, faithful presence in Granby . . . so that the flux and uncertainty all around could be more bravely confronted. Hopelessness waited round every corner because of the scale of human need; the little Church shared the anguish, but also embodied a future hope' (May and Simey 1989).

Witnessing to the Kingdom of God on a challenging estate is of course risky, and for our risk-averse society it's quite counter-cultural. It can prove to be one of the most demanding of all ministries in Britain today. John Vincent has published a series of stories told secretly by ordained ministers to one another, in which they share their fears amid the challenges (Vincent 2003, Chapter 2). We have space only to share a couple:

> There was another stabbing last night. The street opposite is a regular run for the local drug suppliers. Every night, groups of them come together in the stair wells of the block of council flats over the road. Often there are quarrels and frequently shouting and swearing leads to violence. This time the victim was left in a pool of blood.

> A crowd of children and youths climbed onto the roof of the house and started shouting and banging. My wife and I were terrified, and our child was crying . . . We phoned the police again. 'We can't do anything. It's a church house – phone the church', they said. So we telephoned the Diocesan office. 'We have no-one who can come', they said.

These challenges to the ordained are reminders of what it is habitually like for the poor they have chosen to live alongside, who have never had the luxury of living elsewhere. Their stories serve to underline the extraordinary resolve that love demands. The Kingdom of mercy, loving-kindness and justice must surely come 'on earth as it is in heaven', or we are lost. For each and every person living on one of our poorest estates, this prayer is an urgent cry from the heart.

Give us today our daily bread: enough to eat

There is a shift of gear at this point in the Lord's Prayer which is particularly evident in Matthew's version. So far the Prayer has prompted us to honour God as our heavenly Father, to remember that we are all his children and to be alert to our Father's intention to bring in his Kingdom, so that his will may be done on earth as it is in heaven. But now the emphasis changes, and we are confronted by three petitions which spell out how we might actually go about living in that Kingdom day by day and moment by moment. The challenge begins by making us attend to the staple of our daily living – bread.

The Common Greek word *epiousios* – usually translated 'daily' – has only appeared once elsewhere in a now lost scrap of papyrus from the fifth century, so scholars have long debated just what 'daily' bread might mean (Mundle 1975). Jerome and the Nazarene Gospels took the word to mean 'for the coming day', but there are plenty of obvious Greek words readily available that could have been used to say that. Others say that the word refers to 'the final day', when we hope to share the banquet at the end of the age. But the only authority who actually spoke Common Greek as his mother tongue, the early scholar Origen, explains that on the street the word *epiousios* always meant simply 'that which is necessary for life'. This chimes in with today's street-slang use of the word 'bread', and seems to indicate that the original meaning of the petition was simply and starkly, 'give us enough to eat'. I suspect the academics are right to muse about Manna in the Wilderness and the eucharistic overtones of this petition, but I am inclined to think that for the poor who were listening to Jesus teach, this was a simple and heartfelt prayer for a just sharing of the earth's resources – 'please give us enough to eat'.

All over the country, foodbanks are working full tilt in response to people's realistic plea, 'Give us today our daily bread', and the schools that serve our estates, while having in the past been very concerned about their children's poor diet leading to obesity, are now reporting the reappearance of old-fashioned malnutrition due to hunger. Today's supermarkets are stocked to overflowing, but still some mothers have to make a choice between whether their children are kept warm or fed.

It's difficult for most people living in comfort in the UK to understand how this can be. Indeed, this petition that asks God to give us enough to eat sounds simply irrelevant for those who have plenty and who nevertheless say it daily without stopping to question its meaning. During the French Revolution Marie Antoinette, on hearing the poor crying out for bread, uttered the banal response 'let them eat cake' because her horizons were even more limited than our own. But still today many a well-meaning politician and social commentator truly believes that families are able to live on the meagre incomes that the government stipulates – they simply have no idea, since they have never been forced to live on the breadline themselves. From their perspective, the poor seem to be trying to hoodwink the rich. The Lord's Prayer is therefore as much a sign to the rich as to the poor that we should all open our eyes to the realities of the needy. For myself, I have only just learned from my wife that half the clients at our local foodbank are in work. However, working full-time on the minimum wage will today result in a weekly income of about £242, which has devalued since 2008, when in real terms it was worth £255. A person who can only find part-time minimum waged work will only receive £112 a week – less than £6,000 a year. Many of those going to foodbanks will have no cooking facilities at their flat, and they will often be on pre-paid fuel meters, which make them pay more per kilowatt hour than others do. And across the country, we learn from the House of Commons Library that 1,500,000 children are automatically disqualified from free school meals because their parents have found work – even at those abysmal minimum wage levels – and during school holidays all those who do qualify have to go without. As soon as we look at some of the facts, we can understand that many people in the UK have much cause to pray to God that they may be given today their daily bread.

While for the poor the word 'bread' or 'dough' represents money – that which is necessary for life – for the rich money is more likely to be seen as an opportunity for investment. We can certainly see this in the poorer estates, where there are now so few houses in the social housing sector that private letting becomes a lucrative enterprise. Houses can be bought for knock-down prices, let at rentals far above those that the same house would have raised under council ownership, and let to tenants without too much need for maintenance. The tenants are therefore forced to apply for increased housing benefit, which is then handed on to the landlord, thus subsidizing the private sector. Similarly, employers can continue to pay their employees the minimum wage, knowing that the shortfall can be subsidized by government tax-credits. In both cases, the welfare money finishes up in the pockets of the wealthy, while the poor are blamed for increases in the overall welfare budget. It was George who first explained this to me:

> I've lived in this house for years, but the landlords have been changing all the time, and I don't think I've ever actually seen any of them. I've worked it out that over the last five years my rental has gone up by a quarter, even though no repairs are ever done. He knows he'll get it though 'cos I get support for my rent. My wages have gone down, see – made us redundant, then took us all on again on insecure new contracts. The boss just laughs about it and says we've got nothing to worry about, because we'll get tax-credits to make up the loss. But that's easier said than done!

The prayer for bread unmasks a profoundly dysfunctional system which is stacked against the poor, giving the impression of care but lining the pockets of others – reminiscent of the Jerusalem Temple regulations against which Jesus railed (see Luke 19.45–21.7). This is why in the Lord's Prayer the plea for bread is set within the vision of a new Kingdom society, where justice reigns, greed is eradicated and where there is an equitable sharing of life's blessings.

Kingdom values: a compass for Kingdom living

As we have meditated upon the phrases of the Lord's Prayer, they have proved to be a gospel lens through which to look at all we have been learning about poverty from those who live on our social housing estates. The outcome of this theological reflection has been to pull into sharper focus the Kingdom values that crystallize our gospel perspective and so act as markers to Kingdom living. So before we move on to consider other petitions from the Lord's Prayer, it may serve to construct a simple table of the Kingdom values that have been focused thus far, so that we have an *aide-mémoire* for use later in our study. The reader may be content with my following suggestions or prefer to draw together their own.

Table of Kingdom values

Positive Kingdom Values	**Opposing Attitudes**
Our	*Our*
Togetherness as brothers and sisters Mutuality of care	Individualism and separation Exclusion and alienation
Father – Abba	*Father – Abba*
Desire for close relationships Concern for children's flourishing A parent's wish to provide	Distant officialdom Disregard Using others
in heaven	*in heaven*
Transcendence and justice Alert to the special in the ordinary Raising horizons	Surface judgements The drab is sufficient for you Obdurate pessimism
Hallowed be your name	*Hallowed be your name*
Honouring God in all things Respecting the spark of God in others	Treating people as statistics Demonizing and shame

Positive Kingdom Values	**Opposing Attitudes**
Your Kingdom come	*Your Kingdom come*
Extravagant little signs of love Yearning for justice The impossible can be realized	Everyone for themselves Judgementalism Hopelessness
Your will be done, on earth as in heaven	*Your will be done, on earth as in heaven*
Attention to context and place Small actions signifying the Kingdom Action goes together with reflection	One size fits all There is no meaning for us Abstraction or mindless activity
Give us today our daily bread	*Give us today our daily bread*
Just and equal sharing God is on side of the poor Seeing things from below with the poor	Rich are more deserving Using poor to enrich the rich Top-down and trickle-down

5

Kingdom Living

The next petitions of the Lord's Prayer draw our attention to the snares that await us as we challenge the present culture by seeking to lead a Kingdom-oriented life together. Again, we see Jesus going right to the heart of the matter in his prayer, pulling no punches in his challenge to us but nevertheless also offering us ways into deeper awareness of how the Kingdom works. First, he alerts us to our shortcomings but at the same time offers us a most valuable gift, forgiveness.

Forgive us our trespasses: shameful burdens lifted

Sin is, of course, to be found everywhere, but on poor estates it is 'in your face'. Paul Keeble and his family have lived and ministered from a terraced house on a very old estate in Longsight, Manchester for many years. He was suddenly awakened by the overhead thudding of a helicopter which was beaming its searchlight into his backyard, as the police apprehended two armed suspects. The estates in Longsight and nearby Moss Side had a long history of gun crime, centring around the tensions between two notorious gangs, the Longsight Crew and the Gooch Close Gang, and Paul had suddenly been pitched into the fray. At its height in 2006, the annual number of gun-related crimes in south Manchester had reached 120, with 13 deaths in a three-year period, plus numerous woundings. Paul set about challenging all this. With his colleagues, he organized a 'No More!' march and followed that up with the establishment of Carisma, an organization devoted to demonstrating that young people are 'created and valued by God, and should be given viable opportunities to fulfil their God-given potential' (Keeble 2004, p. 104). Paul was clear that forgiveness is not only about setting aside past wrongs but, more importantly, being given ways to begin afresh. Sin is a vicious circle, which comes back round to bite us, unless forgiveness takes sinner and sinned-against together into the possibility of a more positive future.

Paul's colleague Derek Purnell reminds us that for many who live on our worst estates the good news they long to hear concerns escape – to leave the place altogether or else be given the wherewithal to make their existence there more palatable. Derek believes with all his heart that Christians have answers to these yearnings, but again he has no illusions about the realities that chase people away from estate living. All too many find the 'good news' of escape in a bottle or through drugs. Among the young, as we've heard, many find that the awful burdens of their lives are made more bearable by inducing highs through joy riding or violent living. For hope they substitute gambling, and for experiences of transcendence they grasp at anything from pornography to football. Crime rates are shockingly high on some estates, where the sense of togetherness has been fractured, and the fear that many experience can induce long-lasting mental illness. As an urban child, I well remember the numbing daily fear of street attack, and the uplifting relief I felt on being accepted into a street gang. Today, fears like that are even more pronounced, be it of street attack, the loan shark, the drug dealer, the bailiff – and so the fears go on.

One primary school head was clear that because many on the estate find it hard to verbalize their feelings accurately, when confronted by the police or a local government officer, their frustration can make them appear more aggressive than they intend to be. This alienates those who do not understand and can so easily end in tears of exasperation, misunderstanding, or even arrest. She herself was often on the wrong end of parental wrath, but given time for the emotions to calm, it was not unusual for parents to return, seeking a kind of forgiveness, albeit in their own way. Deep down we all long for forgiveness, but our society has long forgotten how to request it or dispense it. Instead of seeking forgiveness we project our sinfulness outward. When God asks Adam why he took the apple, he blames Eve for leading him on. When God then asks Eve why she did that, she blames the snake for leading her on, and the snake from then on is determined to get its own back on them both. God, by contrast, is determined to construct a path back to reconciliation. It is a great pity that the sacrament of Reconciliation, of personal confession with a priest or minister, has fallen out of favour in large parts of the Church, for it encourages personal honesty in a way our wider society does not, and when it is done prayerfully and with integrity, it can prove to be one of the most healing of sacraments. Many a penitent, on hearing those words of forgiveness authoritatively spoken, has broken down in tears of relief and thankfulness. And when in church we confess our sins together, we are owning the fact that it is not only individuals that need forgiveness but whole communities.

A constant source of temptation is, as ever, money. To have too little can lead people to act in ruthless and immoral ways, just as having too much of it can do the same. On the estate, money worries often lead to arguments and family break-up, thrusting tenants into the clutches of loan sharks and payday lenders. Across the globe, it is women who bear the brunt of poverty, and on the estate it is often the woman who is given the almost impossible task of budgeting the meagre household finances. But that also means a heightened risk of her being blamed for the inevitable shortfalls. At the Church of St Martha the Housewife, named by the women of the Broxtowe estate, I spotted a poster showing a woman trapped in a glass jar. The caption read: 'We'll help you break free from domestic violence'.

To pray for the forgiveness of trespasses on the estate is sometimes very difficult when the crimes are so horrendous, but mostly that prayer comes more easily if we know the 'back-story'. We know, for example, that some stoop to theft or burglary simply to feed their families, others just to bring some exhilaration into their lives, while others I know have committed crime in the hope of being put back in prison – the safe haven for those who really cannot cope with estate life. Many clergy tell me they struggle with a dilemma about the alternative ethical codes of their parishioners, for living close to very poor people on a run-down estate does make one question those ethical frameworks in society that are founded more on the value of property than the sacredness of human beings. But forgiveness signals that we should not be chained to the past, whoever's fault it was. Sin is complex, and the Lord's Prayer is helpful in leaving aside analysis for the moment and simply asking for all-encompassing forgiveness.

As we forgive those who trespass against us: mutuality

But talk of sin and forgiveness sounds rather abstract if not fanciful on the estates, where no one would use terms like this naturally. But here our linguistic scholars help us once again by pointing us to the original Aramaic language of the Lord's Prayer, evident in Matthew's version, which talks not about forgiving sins but forgiving debts. Now although I don't hear the word 'sin' mentioned in estate conversations I do repeatedly hear phrases such as 'I'm up to my ears in debt' and 'You owe me one!' Suddenly the Aramaic original makes us more aware that sin has a strongly relational quality – it is not simply something I do but something that makes me indebted to another. My personal sin hurts God, and my societal sins hurt others – there are debts owing all around. And the relational quality of this debt or sin is focused sharply in one of Jesus' parables, where a steward is forgiven a fantastically substantial debt by his master only to go out and imprison someone who owes him a paltry sum (Matt. 18.23–34). We must take care, says Jesus, for just as the master in the story had therefore to punish the steward, so 'my heavenly Father will deal with you unless you each forgive your brother from your heart' (v. 35). Bishop Martin Wharton remembers hearing a knock at his door and, on answering it, confronted by a very large Newcastle City supporter sporting his black and white T-shirt and tattoos. He came right up to Martin, looked him in the eye, and thrust £100 into his hand. 'You'd better come in,' said Martin. It turned out that some years before, the young man had hit rock-bottom, dealing in drugs and abusing others. He had never been off his estate, he had no job and, as he put it, he'd lost his soul. The local parish church had paid for two youth workers for the estate, who had befriended him and encouraged him to take up their offer of a group visit to Peru. There he had joined the team in building a clinic for the destitute, and the experience turned his life around, restoring his self-confidence and convincing him that he had possibilities. He had returned to the UK, trained as a community worker, and now wanted to donate his first £100 towards youth workers to serve the next generation of estate kids. Like the tax-collector Zacchaeus (Luke 19.1–10), being forgiven had transformed him, and he now realized the importance of repaying his debt to those he had abused in the past. One hears many Zacchaeus stories like this on the estates – where a person messes up, but is nevertheless befriended and forgiven, and that changes their life, so that they reach out to others.

Knowing we are forgiven and trusted makes forgiving another person easier, but if that person still persists in doing wilful harm what then are we to do – forget the need for justice? No, we cannot simply ignore the injustice that surrounds our estates, but we must remember that these petitions asking for forgiveness and asking that we may be able to forgive others are given to us by a Jesus who also fights for justice and requires that we join him in that cultural battle to see Kingdom values prevail. So it was that when the rich rulers saw debt as a useful weapon of control over the Palestinian peasants, keeping them in thrall to the Temple and to the Roman authorities, Jesus proclaimed it as an opportunity for forgiveness – a restructuring of the power relations within society. Furthermore, Jesus was not only content to teach this principle but to die for it, saying even from the cross, 'Father, forgive them; they do not know what they are doing' (Luke 23.34). This is a plea for a depth of justice that truly does pass all our limited understanding and demands a generosity that is quite terrifying. The Lord's Prayer therefore calls us to join him in the business of a mutual forgiveness that is full of risk but which is of such power and significance. It is the only way to break into the vicious circle of humanity's injustices once and for all. Because sin and debt is at heart relational, it's forgiveness that is fundamental to the rebuilding of just societal relationships.

Lead us not into temptation: the time of trial

The petition for our daily bread has addressed the needs of the present, while the plea for forgiveness has addressed the chains of the past. Now the Prayer turns its attention to the future – 'lead us not into temptation'. The new head teacher at our estate primary school was explaining to me how difficult it is to convince her children that education will secure their future. As many as 36 per cent have been convinced by TV programmes such as *Britain's Got Talent*, *The Voice* or *X-Factor* that one day they will be discovered and get their big break – so why study? I was taught, as was she, that to escape from poverty the best plan was to work hard at school, but many of her children will know graduates in debt stacking shelves in supermarkets alongside those with no qualifications at all. They themselves prefer a future with no university debts hanging round their necks. The temptation to let schooling sail past them is very strong, but later when the reality bites, and they know themselves to be jobless and penniless, a whole raft of yet more temptations is waiting to fill the vacuum. Some young girls become pregnant in the hope that a baby will bring them a purpose in life, a respected identity as a mother, and someone to care for. Others are tempted by predators to take out high-interest loans, indulge in petty crime, or just drown out their problems with alcohol or drugs. There are many other anaesthetics on offer too – not least daytime TV, which so absorbs some parents that they lose all consciousness of responsibility, sending their children to school unfed. Chris, a Manchester vicar, tells me that since his parish has been offering free breakfasts for local children, their school results have gone from strength to strength. He says that on his estate 'the majority are genuine struggling families, but the others have just dropped out and are lost in gambling on the internet or some other mindless addiction, with a couple of families I know raking in the benefits. Mind you,' he quickly adds,

> we had a claims inspector locally who realized that most of the so-called benefit 'fraud' that he was having to deal with was actually down to honest mistakes with the claims forms. So he brought this to the attention of his managers. He came round here nearly in tears, because they threatened to sack him – they'd said: 'You're not here to give them advice!' But it's clear to me that there are some who are working the system to their own advantage. I'm not sure how far to blame them though when they see their MPs doing the same thing with their expenses. It's quite a temptation when your income is so minimal.

Saying no to temptations such as this is a very real test when the prevailing culture of our society advertises nearly every commodity as a 'must have'. So why try to swim against society's norms?

The New Jerusalem Bible translates this petition in the Lord's Prayer as 'do not put us to the test' (Matt. 6.13), and most of us wonder how we would do if our faith were really tested to the full. Living an overtly Christian life on a social housing estate brings us pretty close to the test, because there is little that is hidden in such an introverted and crammed environment, little pretence that will not be seen through and little opportunity to escape. We certainly don't have the money for 'retail therapy' when we're down, so for many there's not much to lift the spirits. Life is simply a relentless struggle.

When Christ is in the desert being tempted or when he kneels in the Gethsemane garden with sweat like blood dripping from his forehead, this is not a picture of one who is immune to temptation, but a portrait of one who is so overwhelmed by the presence of God that nothing false can divert him from following the values of the Kingdom. The prayer to combat temptation asks for strength not to follow the crowd, but to have the wherewithal to create communities that are not constantly giving in to this culture's temptations but instead living the Kingdom values. In a tempting world we pray that we may pass the test.

Deliver us from evil: the structural nature of sin

When Jesus stares across the City of Jerusalem from the cross he is not only seeing the sins of individuals within it, but knows that there is another dimension to the sin that has crucified him there. It is as if the very city itself, the shortcomings of the Jewish nation and religion, the oppressive slaveries of the Roman Empire, together with the history and structure of the cultures, are all infected with something wrong that is even more insidious than any of the individuals within them – it is sinister and menacing. John the Divine pictures this evil as a Beast, and as it grows in stature the crowd exclaims 'Who can fight against it?' (Rev. 13.4). It's when we notice the buck doesn't stop with anyone in particular, or when whistle-blowers are too frightened to act, that there's every reason to think that evil is infecting the system – the Beast is prowling about. When the poor fail to receive the support that is their due, we might phone the offending department and find that we are treated well and supportively by each individual concerned, and yet we are handed on from one department to the next until we come back around to the supportive person with whom we first spoke, nothing having been achieved. Similarly, some very well-meaning politicians, believing they are acting for the good of society, have been savage in cutting the provision for the poor. It is all too easy to get sucked in by the evil in the structures and unwittingly become its agents – 'Who can fight against it?' Now and again, however, we do see people courageous enough to own what has happened to them and seek to make amends. It was reported by the *Independent* newspaper that Lord Norman Tebbit, once so vehemently critical of foodbanks, decided eventually to visit one and came away extremely impressed and wanting to ask questions about why the poor have to rely on hand-outs, saying: 'I'll have to eat a fair plate of humble pie.' As the newspaper article had it, 'As U-turns go, it was pretty spectacular.' Tebbit had the courage and honesty to own a truth most would prefer not to know.

Sometimes evil is more easy to spot. I went to visit the Darnall Family Development Centre in Sheffield, because I had heard about the astonishing work they had been doing on the estate, helping families to thrive in harsh circumstances. Through 13 years it had grown and won such respect that no fewer than 50 volunteers, many of whom had started out as clients, were now helping to run the centre. But on the very day of my visit their committee had heard that the government cuts will probably close the centre down in order, so they believe, to help redress the country's deficit. The excuse is that recovery will therefore follow, and the benefits of the recovery will then trickle back down to the poor. One thing's for sure – it will help the wealthy regain their financial security, although it has to be noticed that throughout the financial crisis the banks never made a loss, they only depleted their profits. But by the time the poor in Darnall benefit, those children who today rely on the centre will have suffered terribly and will have therefore become needy parents themselves. And as for the trickle-down theory, it was the great monetarist Milton Friedman himself who observed that while the theory is good, it has always been disproved by human history! Ask who will benefit from the closure and we begin to see here an example of evil masquerading as good.

Evil, however, is often even more subtle than this. The Church deserves praise for its long record of care for the needy, but it has often been remarked that while we can pull someone out of a river and feel pleased that their individual life is saved, our elation may make us forget to look further upstream to discover what is pushing the people in in the first place. Most people seeing the incredible commitment and good work done by our foodbanks will rightly applaud, but a critical eye will observe that in a rich country such as ours the very existence of a foodbank should never be necessary, and therefore these projects serve as a clear sign of an inequality and injustice deep in the heart of society. Foodbanks point us quite rightly to the beauty of charity but also alert us to an evil below the surface. Evil seeks to point us to the alleviation of symptoms so that we inadvertently miss the causes. So it was that when New Labour set up the Social Exclusion Unit in 1997 a great deal of emphasis was laid upon the needs of the poor and excluded so that many of us worked hard to see the Unit develop and succeed. But the reports that emanated from it always concentrated on the excluded, the symptom, and never pointed the finger at the cause – the excluders. Similarly, when governments through the years have targeted estates and funnelled money into areas of deprivation we have been right to applaud that investment, but has that blinded us to the fact that the causes of those local problems may have been altogether elsewhere, at a level of society far removed from the estate?

The Bible often personifies this structural evil as the Devil or Satan in order to impress upon us the power and cunning of the evil that seems able to carry us along in these ways. That's why the letter to the Ephesians exhorts us to put on the armour of God since 'we are not contending against flesh and blood, but against the principalities, against the powers, against the world rulers of this present darkness, against the spiritual hosts of wickedness in the heavenly places' (Eph. 6.12, RSV). This striking language helpfully emphasizes the awesome resistance this evil has to human intervention, and therefore the writer implores us to do something – put on the armour of God – for we have a fight on our hands.

Some Christians choose to term this conflict 'spiritual warfare', others 'counter-cultural action' – but, however we talk about it, all agree that it is as well not to tackle such obsessive and powerful forces alone but only in informed, prayerful and supportive groups. Individuals who become isolated, exhausted or under-resourced will be tempted to throw in the towel. Christians must recognize that the consolidation of evil in the deeper workings of society needs to be analysed and confronted, even if our contribution to the battle seems on the face of it so meagre by comparison. For as Eleanor Roosevelt rightly said, 'It is better to light a candle than curse the darkness.'

Yours is the Kingdom: being turned around

Unlike the rest of the Lord's Prayer, the final verses do not actually appear in the Gospel texts at all, but we know they originated during the earliest days of the Church because Christians soon began to end their prayers with a Trinitarian clause, so this non-Trinitarian ending must be very early indeed. There is also a strong possibility that Jesus assumed that his disciples would end the prayer in this way, because in the synagogue an ending of this sort was automatically added in the form of such a doxology – a prayer in praise of God's glory. So with such an ending in place, the Lord's Prayer now finishes in the same way that it began, by addressing God in praise and adoration – always the best way to frame our prayers. This is especially helpful because the last few petitions of the Prayer – to share our bread, to forgive one another's sins, and to deal with evil – are very hard calls and beyond our capacity if left to our own devices. By saying to God, 'yours is the Kingdom', we are now acknowledging that with God 'all things are possible' (Mark 10.27, RSV), and we can adopt an expectant frame of mind. Despite the temptations and the evil, our pessimism slips away and we are left on the tiptoe of expectation, seeing signs of the new Kingdom culture even in the midst of our most drab and dismal estates.

The deprivation tables rank Willenhall as the most deprived area of Coventry, but to visit the estate's church on a Sunday morning you would never think it. Katrina Scott, the parish priest, finds herself surrounded by a lively congregation that is keenly engaged with the issues of the community. The laity take leading roles in the worship, which has a broadly Catholic feel about it. Modern words are used, but the service still follows the pattern that has been prevalent since the very first Christian centuries. The sermon carefully unpacks the Bible passage for the week in terms of our daily lives and the issues of the day, and the congregation sings lustily the traditional hymns and the more modern worship songs. After the service, amid the chatter, coffee and biscuits are shared between those who have been worshipping and those who now pop in to join them from the Community Forum, for this congregation doesn't try to do everything itself but reaches out to join other people and organizations who are giving of themselves to help the community thrive. Although the congregation is not large nor any longer sprightly, it looks decidedly outward from itself into the community around, and ironically this has given them a stronger sense of their own identity, and those around them in the community affirm that. One local woman said to me: 'Ah, they keep the light burning in Willenhall, you know.' As much as we bemoan the tough realities and the many seeming failures of our Christian presence on the estates, we also recognize glimpses everywhere of the power of God's Kingdom, alive and vibrant.

Sometimes the Kingdom manifests itself in a very personal way. So although his life is still somewhat chaotic, Terry feels things are turning around for him. The gang he used to run with have beaten him up since he started to go to church, but as he says himself: 'That's nothing new for me. But this time it felt different. Now I know God's got his eye on it all. I know he wants me to be OK. I didn't used to think God was interested in any of us round here, but now, well, it feels different somehow. I even get up properly in the mornings now.' It may not sound much, but Terry knows that his life is being turned slowly around by a realization that God's Kingdom includes people like himself.

But there are lots of other influences that are vying for Terry's allegiance. When like Terry we have, through a process generations long, become a victim of harsh circumstances, a common response can either be to play the role of martyr or else to engage in arbitrary violence and aggression. He tells me that he has played out both roles during his short life. But in addition to this, Terry – like everyone else – is being moulded by advertisements, peer pressures and the subtle expectations of our culture, to believe that life is really about getting as much as we can and consuming all the 'must have' products of the market place. Ben Drew, the rapper known as Plan B, is an acknowledged authority on daily life on London's toughest estates. In response to the 2011 street riots he says:

> I understand the frustration. The rioters went out and fought for what they believed in: widescreen TVs, DVDs and trainers! Every day they watch TV they're told to buy these things, and that if you don't have them people will look down on you. A lot of kids just saw an opportunity – a shop that was smashed in, that has the trainers they wanted. But those trainers are an

> easy fix for now. They're not going to change your life (*Big Issue* 2012, p. 19).

When we pray 'Yours is the Kingdom' we are affirming which culture it is that we wish to be conformed to – the 'let's snatch everything we can grab' culture or God's Kingdom of inclusion, justice and celebration.

The power is yours: acting serenely

The most profound depiction of the nature of God's power is to be found in the doctrine of God's Holy Trinity. For here is revealed to us how three persons, equal in power and authority, can yet be one in unity of purpose, action and generosity. If we are truly made in God's image, we should endeavour to reflect this partnering mode of life, never acting selfishly nor imperiously, but always incarnationally alongside those for whom we have concern. This dynamic intertwining of persons, always mutually deferential, never denying the authority and power of the other, but always moving forward together for the good of the other, is the model upon which all our human relationships should be based. This redefining of power lies at the very heart of the Prayer's challenge to our society.

A woman priest, living on a very tough estate, says her prayers every evening in church, leaving the doors open. The local youngsters have taken to joining her, lighting candles, larking about, and just sometimes taking it seriously. One evening she saw a large lad attacking a smaller boy, and she rushed across the church to his defence by putting herself between the two. The lad was not deterred and struck out at her, and as she sought to defend herself against his barrage, she pushed him back and thus saved the small boy from being seriously hurt. But the larger lad's response was to call the police, accusing her of attacking him. The police took her to the cells for interrogation, pressing her to say that she had acted in self-defence. But she knew that if she admitted that, the older lad would then be charged and prosecuted. So she decided to remain silent. She therefore received an unpleasant formal caution, and the child protection unit put this courageous priest on to a course of corrective training! She told no one what she had done to protect the boys. She continues to pray in the open church, and the youngsters love to join her, although her congregation are now too scared of them to pray alongside her. Several forms of power were operating through the process of this event, not least her powerful intervention during the lad's abuse of his power. This was followed by her arrest at the hands of the official powers. That in turn had given her the power to blight the life of one of those she was seeking to serve, but she decided instead to make an offering of her powerlessness so that God's power to heal could be given opportunity. But hers was the power of love that came at a price – but whenever did powerful love like this come at no cost?

When the welfare state first came into being, it was hailed by the Archbishops of the Church of England as the nearest thing to the Kingdom of God that had been seen in British political history. How miraculous it must have seemed after the evil darkness of two devastating world wars that political power was now going to be used to care for all citizens, regardless of their wealth and background. Much later, in the mid-1980s, it was Michael Heseltine who started to fly the flag for the run-down inner cities of the north of England, using his power and influence to effect significant advances for those areas. Again, how refreshing it was, after many years of decline in the standards of public housing, to read the words of John Prescott: 'There is a backlog of renovation in the local authority housing stock and we have therefore provided an additional £3.6 billion to deliver improvements in 1.5 million council homes.' These three examples of those in power taking compassionate initiatives warm the heart. They remind us that power can be a very positive energy for good and a vehicle for the working of the Holy Spirit within political and economic structures. The structures of a society can be used to bring about remarkably good outcomes, but those same structures must not be allowed to grow beyond their competence nor be subverted by unscrupulous powers.

A Kenyan friend, Guti Dan, puts the same warning in another way: 'Are you an eagle? . . . the sound of the eagle does not excite the chicken!' If power is used to promote Kingdom outcomes, we can glory in it, but the poor, like the chicken, are on the alert to know if power is being used to enable or ravage. That is why Kingdom living demands that we analyse all uses of power from the perspective of the weak, and remember its divine provenance.

The glory is yours: looking up!

These final phrases of the Lord's Prayer assure us that despite all the challenges, with God everything is redeemable, even the deep structures of society, be they so often infected by evil. For even the structures originate as a gift of God to us, for where would we be without a system of law, a market place, education, systems of house building, and so on? No modern human society would prove sustainable without structures. This is why the writer of the letter to the Colossians declares that all things were created through and for Jesus. 'He exists before all things and in him all things hold together' (Col. 1. 17). In this verse, the word we translate as 'hold together' is the Greek word *sunistemi*, from which we derive our word 'systematize'. So the Bible leads us to appreciate that the systems that surround us are not there by mistake, but exist to give creation an ordered pattern of life and possibility.

From time to time the structures will work well. The family will rejoice in their child's progress at the estate school and cheer and clap at the prize-giving. The cramped household will be found the perfect accommodation, the young girl will be placed on an apprenticeship scheme, and the estate football team will rejoice at its mixed ethnicity. The glory of God will be revealed. But even when the structures have broken down or work against those they were meant to serve, they remain redeemable. That is why the letter to the Colossians goes on to tell how Jesus has thrown the spotlight on to the structures, stripping and unmasking them so that we can see again what they were meant to be – our tools and not our masters. At his crucifixion, Jesus has made a public spectacle of them by placarding their evil from the cross for all to see. The Romans were fond of their triumphant processions into the city after a great victory when the vanquished would be relegated to the end of the procession in chains. So the letter to the Colossians pictures Jesus as having 'stripped the sovereignties and the ruling forces, and paraded them in public, behind him in his triumphal procession' (Col. 2.15). The Lamb has triumphed over the Beast, allowing the structures of society still to function, but now fully stripped of their mythology, and back in their proper place in the order of creation – at the back of the procession, there to serve. With this Kingdom frame of mind, we can learn to appreciate how the job centre, the benefits system, the local authority, or even the market economy, are there to serve a good purpose while at the same time acknowledging the profound abuses, and fighting to end them. For by exposing the fault-lines of a bad system new approaches become more attractive and realizable. As Leonard Cohen's song has it, 'There's a crack in everything – that's where the light gets in.'

It is counter-intuitive to expect to find God's glory particularly evident in poorer communities, but it may be so because in such areas there is little of humanity's vainglory to obscure it. The environment has often been rubbished, and the architecture has none of the 'wow factor' of the modern city sky-scrapers, but against that bleak backdrop, God's glory shines out even more brightly. I have always looked forward to participating in worship in back-street estate churches, because in every case, even when the service has not been very well managed and the building has been draughty and lacklustre, I can honestly say it has always brought me closer to the presence of God in the midst. Is it because of the stark reality of the situation in which the worship is set, or is it because of its simplicity and the unaffected devotion of those attending? I simply do not know. But it is as if in the draughty hall the curtain of the Temple is in shreds and God is most assuredly with his people. No one has been polished of their reality on entry, and it's very clear that we are all depending on one another and on God. On our estates, worship is an essential ingredient of life, for by praising God's glory it counters the negativities and despondency that so often drag us down. And from that worshipping experience of God in the midst, worshippers gain power and confidence to praise God in their daily estate lives, whatever the challenges.

For ever and ever: living in God's constancy

The final phrase of the Prayer – 'for ever and ever, Amen' – is important but easily overlooked. It brings home to us that we are operating within the context of something that is so much bigger than ourselves, for alongside all that we experience and all that we do, there is another plane of being, intersecting with our own and giving it meaning. We enact the Eucharist of bread and wine in the back room of a council house and suddenly realize that we are participating in the eternal Eucharist of thanksgiving in heaven. We are living our lives within the context of the 'ever and ever', so even our small and mundane offerings can be sacramental of that eternal reality. This means that even our small toddlers' group on the estate may be pointing to, and even participating in, God's eternal heavenly Kingdom. Our small events of sharing become symbolic of the eternally sharing Holy Trinity; our small protest against an injustice can signify and share in the eternal justice of God; our welcome of newcomers into the warmth of a church gathering can be indicative of the generous hospitality of God to us, we who fail God so regularly. So our time-constrained lives are put in the context of the divine eternity – 'for ever and ever' – and we see the hidden significance of even the most modest act of faith. We ourselves become part of God's eternity.

On some poor estates it is an act of faith just to carry on. During an enactment of the Stations of the Cross we were all gathered around a picture of that moment when Jesus falls for the third time under the weight of the cross on his way to crucifixion. He is blooded and in agony. As we stood and pondered the scene, one of the congregation cried out: 'For heaven's sake just stay down!' He understood how it can feel to be on the floor scorned and abused by a gang of bullies. I never cease to be amazed at the resilience and perseverance of poor people, when they are knocked down so often. And the rest of society seems to act like those Roman crucifixion soldiers who jeer at those who are down and accuse them of not having sufficient aspiration to pull themselves up and do better. But our study shows that it would be more fitting to feel inspired by the poor than to jeer when we see what they are able to handle in their day-to-day struggle to survive. Managing to survive against all the odds is one thing in which many poor people take great pride. Despite lack of resources or support, the little church stoically opens every Sunday morning. Those who close down such churches without being sensitive to the locals are doing much more than closing a building. They are being contemptuous of what those churches symbolize – the survival gifts of the poor.

Many a poor housing estate gives the impression that it was once a land of promise, but it was a promise never fulfilled. It was to counteract this mindset that the little congregation at the Church of the Epiphany on the Gipton Estate worked hard to make its carol service a success. And to their surprise they had 500 people from the estate attend! Now they host concerts, shows, a little community garden for the long-term unemployed, together with cooking classes for mums and dads – all intended to help sustain a healthy future for the community. The vicar grinned at me and remarked, 'God's not just passing through Gipton, he's here *for ever and ever*!' I could only reply – 'Amen!'

We have taken time to meditate upon each phrase and petition of the Lord's Prayer – this Kingdom Prayer that Christians around the world say every day – and we have done this in the company of voices from the poor estates. This perspective has prompted us to unearth new insights and review our former understandings of the Prayer, its origins, and of those surrounding Jesus as he taught them to use it. Hopefully this has inspired us with a growing appreciation that God has much to teach us from the perspective of those who experience poverty, and given us a more ready appetite to confront its injustices. Prayer in turn has shone a light on our society's rather distanced and sometimes negative view of poor people and led us to focus the Kingdom values that will help to guide us as we continue our endeavour. Again, at the end of this chapter, I have tabulated a simple *aide-mémoire* to help us in that undertaking.

So with those values helping us to steer our Kingdom course, and with a deeper appreciation of what the poor have to teach us, we are now better prepared to ask our question in earnest: 'What does Jesus really mean when he says, "blessed are you who are poor"?'

Table of Kingdom values

Positive Kingdom Values	**Opposing Attitudes**
Forgive us our sins	*Forgive us our sins*
Fresh start always possible Some sinned-against, not just sinners Escape is not always honest	We are all stuck Do not be merciful Just drop out
As we forgive those who sin against us	*As we forgive those who sin against us*
Acknowledging debts are mutual Transform our unjust culture	Projecting our guilt Conform to expectation
Lead us not into temptation	*Lead us not into temptation*
Liberation from enslaving culture Power to prevail	Staying locked in Giving in
Deliver us from evil	*Deliver us from evil*
Clarity about the hidden structures Working for awareness	Accepting face values Glossing over problems

Positive Kingdom Values	**Opposing Attitudes**
Yours is the Kingdom	*Yours is the Kingdom*
Expecting lives to be turned around Resisting the culture of smash and grab	Keeping to stereotypes Take what you can where you can
Yours is the power	*Yours is the power*
Using power compassionately Trinity-like mutual sharing	Strongest wins Going it alone
The glory is Yours	*The glory is Yours*
Using structures wisely God-centred worship	Letting structures use us Church-centred worship
For ever and ever	*For ever and ever*
Trust in God's enduring commitment Small faithful actions signifying heaven	Fear of the future Overwhelmed into inaction

6

The Challenge of the Beatitudes

What is it to be blessed?

In the day-to-day language of the estate we might expect to hear the word 'blessed' used as a mild expletive to express annoyance and exasperation rather than as a form of affirmation. But in the New Testament we find Jesus using it to tell the poor that they are endowed with God's especial favour. They are venerated, privileged and protected because God has a special concern for them, even if they have not realized it. When Jesus in the famous passage we call the Beatitudes tells them they are blessed, the word used there is not to be confused with another word, *eulogetos*, which is also translated as 'blessed' in various other places in the New Testament. Our word is a translation of the beautiful-sounding word *Makarios*! The *eulogetos* blessing was something usually only pronounced, as for example in Deuteronomy 28.1 and 15, on condition that whoever received the blessing would undertake certain required tasks. But Jesus says nothing of that sort here. The typical *eulogetos* blessing seems to have originated at a very early date, but *Makarios* blessedness is only developed in much later Jewish literature such as the books of Sirach, Daniel and Tobit. In this case, the person over whom this blessedness was pronounced was being assured of future blessings when at last the Kingdom would come. But by the time of Jesus things had moved much further on, and some contemporary rabbis were using the term to signify the present blessedness of things and people. When we look at the Beatitudes very carefully, which we will do in a moment, it's very clear that Jesus is talking about the poor being blessed and receiving the Kingdom here and now – 'the Kingdom of God *is* yours!' Jesus seems to be saying *Makarios* to signify that although the fullness of the blessing will be realized when the Kingdom comes in all its totality, until then transparent glimpses of it will be realized even now in the lives of the poor. As Professor Ulrich Becker puts it when writing about this passage, its 'futuristic character is not to be understood in the sense of consolation and subsequent recompense. The promised future always involves a radical alteration of the present' (Becker 1975, p. 217). So as Jesus pronounced the poor 'blessed', he was not pretending that they were not still experiencing poverty, hunger and sorrow, but he was affirming that from now on an abundance of Kingdom experiences will overwhelm that ugliness, and when the Kingdom comes in all its glory, poverty will be vanquished for ever, and the full blessings of joy and happiness will be theirs.

A momentous event

To some extent, we've already touched on what some of those blessings might be, as the poor have helped us discern Kingdom values during our reflections on the words of the Lord's Prayer. But to draw nearer to understanding just what Jesus meant we must look carefully now at this provocative and tantalizing statement – the first in a series of extraordinary assertions that have become known as the Beatitudes. Luke and Matthew both give us reports of the Sermon, but with interesting variations that we will address later. But first let us see how Luke frames his account of this crucial teaching. We will find it in Luke 6.20:

> Then fixing his eyes on his disciples he said:
> How blessed are you who are poor:
> the kingdom of God is yours.

Luke makes it clear that this sermon is of the very greatest consequence by telling us that Jesus first goes up into a mountain to pray through the night after which he gathers his disciples together and selects 12 of them (Luke 6.12). His contemporaries would of course have connected such a bold action with the stories they knew from childhood about the establishment of the Jewish nation. They had learned that they were the chosen people of God, organized into 12 tribes around a covenant law of the Ten Commandments that God had given to Moses on the mountain. So in designating these 12 leaders on the mountain, Jesus was boldly inaugurating a new Kingdom to be based presumably on a new covenant that Jesus would now share with them. In naming these 12 disciples Luke makes an interesting observation when he says Jesus now 'called them apostles' (v. 13). The word 'disciple' means 'learner', but in those days the apostle was simply an ambassador – one who is sent out with a message. The Gospels, however, often use the two words almost interchangeably which makes us realize how well they understood that those who teach and proclaim the Good News would also need to be learners. But additionally, here the distinction is highlighted, as if to say that the teaching that is to follow and the new Kingdom that Jesus is inaugurating cannot be contained within his immediate discipleship group of followers, but from now on must be proclaimed and broadcast far and wide. The former Chief Rabbi Jonathan Sachs was once asked what he thought of Christians, to which he graciously replied that while the Jewish people had treasured their faith, it took the Christian Church to take the faith outward into the world as a missionary movement. The 12 are certainly reminiscent of the old 12 tribes of Israel, but from now on they are also to be apostolic missionaries for that new Kingdom.

Luke then goes on to make it clear that this foundational event and the crucial teaching that is to follow is especially for the poor. He does this by telling us that Jesus immediately led the 12 down the mountain on to more level ground, where a vast crowd of disciples had gathered to hear his teaching and open themselves up to his healing touch. The impression we have from the text is that this was not a genteel gathering but a vast crowd of very ordinary people – indeed the biblical scholar Anthony Harvey (Harvey 1990) has no doubt that these people would have been, as he put it to me, 'on the breadline'. It is at this point that Jesus becomes very earnest with them by 'fixing his eyes upon them', and he then shares with them the first of his Beatitudes. In this way Luke has built up to the Sermon with great care, underlining how critical this teaching is to the whole of Jesus' ministry. It has the authority of a new Ten Commandments, issued in the company of the leaders of the newly inaugurated nation, and must not be ignored. Matthew similarly stresses how important the Beatitudes are by having Jesus preaching while still actually on the mountain, surrounded by the crowd, placing the Beatitudes at the very beginning of a long series of instructions for a Kingdom life. The two evangelists, each in their own way, are emphasizing that we must attend to the teaching that follows with the utmost seriousness, even though we will find it challenging in the extreme.

We can imagine the peasant crowd listening very attentively to hear what Jesus was about to say, and how flabbergasted they must have been to hear that this crucial sermon was all about them – the poor! They are to be the subject of the greatest sermon ever preached.

Understanding their poverty

It is very instructive for us to take account of the carefully crafted structure of the Beatitudes for it gives us an insight into how well Jesus understood just what poverty is. The first Beatitude is the key to all the others. With it, Jesus states his case boldly and then follows it with three other statements that unpack the first. In this way, he describes the poor as hungry, sorrowful and abused – precisely, as we've seen, the three elements that make the poor's situation so unbearable. In the first Beatitude he simply names his listeners as the poor, but in the second, 'blessed are you who are hungry now', he alerts us to one aspect of that deprivation – the sheer lack of resources essential to human flourishing. The next Beatitude, 'blessed are you who are weeping now', focuses on what poverty can do to the human spirit, and the last, 'blessed are you when people hate you', reminds us of all that we have learned about how the poor are shut out, residualized and demonized by society.

By analysing poverty into its several components like this, Jesus indicates that to think of poverty as simply a lack of money is totally to miss the point. From his experience of living as one of the poor he presents poverty as a complex dynamic of forces. It has taken scholars a long time to reach this same conclusion, as Bryant Myers explains in his recent book *Walking with the Poor* (2011, pp. 113–32). Myers analyses poverty as a dynamic of deficit, estrangement, diminishment and lack of access – as a disempowering system that reduces people's freedom to grow – and here in the Beatitudes Jesus similarly characterizes poverty as a multi-faceted disempowerment.

I have made the assumption that the last three Beatitudes flow easily from the first, but many Bible scholars have argued differently.[1] They have assumed the final Beatitude, 'blessed are you when people hate you', to be the early Church's addition, created in the context of its later persecution to affirm the blessedness of its martyrs. But our estate experience attests, and recent New Testament scholarship testifies, that abuse and exclusion are and always have been part and parcel of the experience of poverty. We have learned that today as always, the poor are treated as something apart, sometimes even residualized and housed separately from the rest of society. They are reviled as being different and not part of the larger society, laughed at and scorned so that society can have an excuse to ignore the relationship between their own wealth and the poor lives of those they seek to distance themselves from. So it is that the unity of the four Beatitudes stands, requiring us to address poverty as Jesus does, as a complex nexus of factors and not just a lack of money, as fundamental as that is.

Jesus' understanding of this complexity is born of his first-hand experience, but also he stands in a Jewish tradition that never saw poverty simplistically. In the Hebrew Scriptures there are at least five words that we can translate as 'the poor', and each one of them draws out a particular aspect of that condition. *Ani* stresses

1 See the arguments set out by David Mealand, 1980, *Poverty and Expectation in the Gospels*, London: SPCK, pp. 61–3.

that the poor are humiliated, *anaw* that they are made humble, *dal*, they are made weak, *ebyon* that they must beg, and so on. In addition to this, we need to remember that when the Hebrew people inherited the Promised Land each tribe and person received their God-given portion of it, and later a divine Jubilee law was instituted (Lev. 25), which stipulated that at the end of every seventy-times-seven years anyone who had been disinherited of their rightful portion, through debt or misfortune, would have it returned.[2] So the poor knew that they should pray fervently to God so that their portion would be justly restored to them, and the rich in turn knew that they were obliged to give alms, because God had from the first stipulated that the wealth of the land be equitably shared. So their belief (*credo*) in Yahweh, whose land and wealth it all ultimately was, could be signalled by their willingness to repay in alms what they owed (*creditum*), not simply to the poor but ultimately to God! And the expectation that the poor would therefore turn to God in prayer for this restoration resulted in Jews using the word 'poor' to mean not only those who had nothing, but those who fervently prayed. So in Hebrew, all these words for the poor had become underscored by these additional religious meanings (Anderson 2013). When a century before Christ's birth scholars translated the Hebrew Scriptures into Greek they mainly used just two Greek words to render all those Hebrew words: the first, *penes*, meaning a person of limited means, and *ptochos*, referring to a beggar or someone who was oppressively poor. It is significant therefore that informed by Jesus' teaching, the Gospels resoundingly stress the economic disempowerment of the poor by consistently opting for *ptochos*, the much tougher and harsher of the two words. So when Matthew, writing for Jewish readers, touches on those Hebrew additional meanings by having Jesus say 'blessed are the poor in spirit', he nevertheless stresses their actual physical poverty by still using

2 For a full explanation of the Jubilee codes, see Laurie Green, 1997, *Jesus and the Jubilee: The Kingdom of God and Our New Millennium*, London and Sheffield: Jubilee 2000 and UTU Press, New City Special No. 11.

that tough and strident word, *ptochos* – he is still talking about people who have nothing but has incorporated some of those Hebrew meanings too. Luke (chapter 6), however, writes for readers who would know little of that Hebrew background and so keeps to the essential nub of Jesus' statement – Blessed are the Poor.

Unlike Matthew, Luke offers us an intriguing juxtaposition of four Beatitudes and four parallel Woes and sets them out in the following way (my paraphrasing):

- 'You who are poor are blessed' (v. 20).
  The rich have had it (v. 24).
- 'If you're hungry, you will be satisfied' (v. 21).
  The full will go hungry (v. 25).
- 'If you're crying, you will laugh' (v. 21).
  Those laughing will cry (v. 25).
- 'If they hate you, you will be rewarded' (vv. 22–23).
  Celebrities will be proved false (v. 26).

This clear parallel structure was a common feature of Jewish writing, and it serves to heighten the impact of each Beatitude by setting against it a corresponding Woe for the rich. Together the whole composition says quite boldly that while the rich look after themselves, the poor who do not have the wherewithal to fend for themselves are blessed by God with riches of much deeper and lasting value. We can only imagine just how this carefully crafted sermon would have excited the crowd with its promise of justice at last!

We can also see from the close parallel structure of the Beatitudes and Woes that Luke's Jesus fully understood there to be a strong connection between the two opposing states. In other words, the poverty of the poor and the wealth of the rich are connected. It is not just coincidence that the rich are wealthy and quite incidentally that the poor are poor. They are both symptoms of the one system of inequality, and it is maintained by those who will according to the sermon have to pay the price. Myers describes today's rich as those who believe that without their controlling hand the world would descend into chaos and they assume, he says, that their property and power are therefore their entitlement as controller. So just as it is necessary for the poor to know they are blessed and so released from believing themselves to be worthless nobodies, so also the rich must be changed so that they 'relinquish their god complexes and employ their gifts for the sake of all human beings rather than using their gifts as a source of power and control' (Myers 2011, p. 178). Our study has taught us that this systemic connection between poverty and wealth is rarely acknowledged, but the sermon's parallel and oppositional form makes it crystal clear to the wealthy and to the poor alike that they are as they are because of one another. Release for one will mean release for the other. As the Lord's Prayer taught us, debt and forgiveness are mutual and salvation can be shared.

God's radical reversal

Having set out so succinctly the nature of poverty, Jesus then sharpens the focus in the second half of each Beatitude. He proclaims in stunning terms that God is introducing a radical reversal of fortunes. In each case, the predicament of the poor will be turned around – they shall be fed, they shall laugh, they shall be counted among the prophets! In our estate Bible study group Tom was amazed: 'You know I've heard this bit before in church, but I never really heard it. Perhaps I'm a bit slow, but this means that Jesus is telling us it's not always got to be like this. Everything's going to change! He's a bit of a revolutionary, isn't he!' Rarely are the poor given opportunity to hear this radical edge to Jesus' teaching.

Some of these radical ideas seem to have evolved from earlier Hebrew insights to which Jesus has given a new and revolutionary twist. For example, the book of Psalms is composed of five sub-divisions or books, the first being a Davidic section that begins with the Beatitude: 'Blessed is the man who walks not in the counsel of the wicked' (Ps. 1.1, RSV), and ends similarly in Psalm 41 with another, 'Blessed is he who considers the poor'

(Ps. 41.1, RSV). And if we read carefully, we begin to see that the whole of this first book of Psalms makes it clear that the two Beatitudes are one and the same – you are blessed if you obey God's ordinances, and you do that by caring for the poor and needy! As one Old Testament scholar, J. C. McCann, explains (1996, p. 847): 'If Psalms 2—40 have made anything clear, it is that God considers the oppressed. Thus those who are open to God's instruction and God's leading, those who live under God's rule, will also "consider the poor".' But the first of Jesus' Beatitudes takes this insight a giant step further, when it proclaims not only that those who care for the poor are blessed, but that the poor themselves are blessed. Now this is new, since throughout the Hebrew Scriptures, while it is considered that giving alms to the poor is an act of the blessed, and indeed that charity is a blessing for the poor, nowhere would they go so far as to say that the poor are already blessed in their own right! The poor are always viewed as objects of others' charity and not as subjects of their own history. But it is clear that Jesus' revolutionary intention is that the poor shall play a crucial role in the Kingdom he is inaugurating. They are the context in which his ministry develops, and they are the first hearers of the gospel. Even at his birth it was to be poor shepherds who were the first to hear the news, and now in the Beatitudes the poor learn that they are the children of the promise – they are blessed, affirmed and empowered for their particularly important role in pointing to the Kingdom of God. While Jesus' teaching and his signs are being attacked by the wealthy and influential, these poor disciples are rallying to him for healing and receiving instruction and teaching, so that they may play their special part in the Kingdom. The poor just seem to get it! Perhaps they feel free to follow him so enthusiastically because they stand outside the power structures and therefore have nothing to lose if those structures are overthrown. Perhaps it's because they can see that this man is actually addressing their immediate needs and has some long-term answers to offer. But while Jesus is no threat to the poor, he is a threat to the powerful because his every word seems to be demolishing the foundations of their power. They have built their house upon sand, and Jesus is stirring up a storm that will knock it down (Matt. 7.24–27).[3]

If we try to imagine the scene – peasants crowding forward straining to hear, taking a moment aside from lives of fatigue and hunger to hear this extraordinarily charismatic man proclaiming that they, the poor, are blessed and will inherit the Kingdom – it begins to register with us that this sermon is turning out to be an empowering rallying call to commitment and action. If they follow this man, they are being assured of a transformation in their lives and fortunes. I asked Sister Anne, an Anglican Benedictine nun at the convent I serve, what she made of this Bible passage, and she, who devotes every hour of her life to living with the Beatitudes, observed that the parallel nature of the Sermon and its clarion call to a revolutionary reversal in society takes us once again into the upside-down world of the Magnificat (Luke 1.46–55). Mary's song is similarly a revolutionary cry for a reversal of all the societal attitudes we take for granted, with a strong emphasis on how the rich and powerful will be put down from their honoured places when the Kingdom comes, and how the poor will be raised up. When Henry Martyn arrived in India in 1805 to be chaplain to the East India Company, he was not allowed to share Mary's Magnificat song with the local Indians for fear they might take her revolutionary words seriously! And today when we compare Mary's challenging song with the strident words of the Beatitudes, we have every reason to assume that she had shared her very revolutionary thinking with Jesus as he grew up, for the burden of her song has so much in common with his Kingdom preaching.[4] In the Beatitudes and Woes, Jesus is not suggesting evolutionary or gentle changes in the organization of our lives, but a radical reversal and reorientation towards Kingdom values. The Sermon is a wake-up call to us all, designed to bring us to a

3 See also the essays in Archbishop Sentamu's collection, *On Rock or Sand? Firm Foundations for Britain's Future* (Sentamu 2015).

4 Some scholars argue from a study of the archaeological evidence and other socio-economic evidence that Mary's family were of decidedly revolutionary stock. My own studies in Sepphoris near Nazareth have led me to agree. (See, for example, Sawicki 2000.)

decision about which direction we now intend our life journey to take. His sermon is a provocative confrontation which throws down the gauntlet and demands that we choose.

And yet for all this, Jesus is no rabble-rouser but, on the contrary, exhibits an extraordinary depth of sensitivity and compassion for his audience. Throughout the sermon he affirms the poor but never condones the poverty that holds them captive. I've noticed a subtle temptation for those who work alongside the poor to boast of the poverty of their area, and at the macro level whole nations advertise themselves as low-wage and non-unionized in order to attract investment, and the poverty of estates is sometimes placarded in order to attract funds. But on the estates we are constantly aware how angry and insulted tenants feel on hearing their locality disparaged and denigrated in this way. We've heard that many poor people don't go to the foodbank or apply for their due benefits because they do not wish to be branded as incompetent or lazy, and even if they agree among themselves that their area is not up to much, they are still offended and upset to hear others talking about it in that way. Jesus never dwells on sufferings or deprivations to stimulate generosity and piety among the rich. He sees nothing commendable about poverty in itself and refuses to accept that anyone should be enslaved by it. On the contrary, he seems very happy that some have funds that they share – he is even content to rely on the wealth of his female disciples Mary Magdalene, Joanna and Susanna to fund his mission (Luke 8.2–3), and he promises a banquet in heaven for all who follow him (e.g. Matt. 22.1–10). He has no love of poverty and wants the poor to be liberated from its obscenity, remaining ever sensitive to the feelings the poor have about their predicament.

He also shows remarkable sensitivity in not talking *about* the poor in his sermon, but he always directly addresses them – 'Blessed are you who are poor!' Too often the poor are reduced to the status of statistics or objects of concern, but Jesus treats them as companions, capable of making decisions about their lives despite the heavy restrictions that their poverty places upon them. At that time, the poor were assumed to be idiots, uneducated and unkempt folk who were not worthy to be addressed directly. The

Roman Juvenal was typical in suggesting, 'If you are poor you are a joke . . . what a laugh if several patches betray frequent mending!' (Juvenal 1999, p. 41). But Jesus is altogether revolutionary in treating the poor as responsible adults with serious options for behaviour and capable of receiving complex teaching, as we shall see as our study progresses.

The Kingdom challenge

This sensitivity and respect for the competence and maturity of the poor allows him to offer them a very costly and demanding option – the opportunity to be in the vanguard of the Kingdom. If they grasp the challenge to follow him, he promises them a cross (Matt. 16.16–24), and being on the poorest estates alongside the poor brings that cross into very sharp relief indeed. There we pray that we will not be 'brought to the time of trial' in an environment that can be raw and the choices stark, the temptations great and the possibilities for mistakes and tears of grief manifold. The biblical desert had qualities not dissimilar to our poor estates where the dangers and the desolation are equally appalling. The morbidity rates of the poor are alone terrifyingly high – just as in the biblical desert where survival was at a premium. But the people of the Bible returned to the desert, that place of demons and blight, to be stripped down and tested, only to find themselves being met there by their God, for there in that place they were brought face to face with their rudimentary selves, uncluttered by pretences or superficiality, dependent for their very lives on him who alone could supply their deepest needs – and so it can be in the poor housing estate. And yet I remember being lucky enough to be in the desert during a rare rainfall, suddenly surrounded by the miracle of a profusion of tiny flowers bursting into life. What seemed so dead proved suddenly to be alive.

Chrissie told me:

> I can't explain it to you, bishop, but before I became a Christian I used to curse this place. I've lived in this flat for I don't know

> how long and never saw it as a place I wanted to be. The things I remember I had to do in that room – well, you know, being on the game was not nice. But with Jesus around the place, so to speak, it feels kinda good. It feels clean and lovely.

The estate still presents its brutal temptations, but now that she knows God is alongside, Chrissie feels blessed to take up a cross and follow him.

So while being very sensitive to his friends the poor, Jesus also respects them highly enough to offer them this very challenging role as the vanguard of the Kingdom, for Kingdom living is challenging even for those who are used to the desert of tough estate life. For example, as we've learned, many have been made aggressively inward-looking and defensive, so that Jesus' message of the generous inclusion of all God's children can prove a very significant threat and a bridge too far. It was in the synagogue at Nazareth that, according to Luke, Jesus first began to make clear that the Kingdom was to be radically different from what any of his contemporaries may have expected. He took the scroll of the prophet Isaiah and read the passage from chapter 61, which sets out some of the markers of the Kingdom – release of captives, recovery of sight for the blind, and freedom for the oppressed – all good news for the poor. In some ways, Jesus was doing with the Hebrew Scripture what we have sought to do by discovering Kingdom markers in the Lord's Prayer. He then told his hearers that this was all now fulfilled in their presence, but then went on to explain that this new dispensation would, against all expectation, be radically inclusive of all the poor and oppressed, regardless of gender, nationality or ethnicity (Luke 4.25–27), and at this we're told, 'everyone in the synagogue was enraged. They sprang to their feet and hustled him out of the town' (v. 28). Tell the original tenants of the estate to welcome in Eastern Europeans or Asian families, and some will use the most racist terms. Jesus tells us that the poor are blessed but this is not to say that all those who are poor will appreciate those blessings, claim that inheritance, or even act in accordance with the Kingdom values. The poor need to hear the good news of their blessing just as much as those who are not poor need to accept it, but there is no guarantee that any of us will respond. Good news for the poor is that they start their Kingdom journey streets ahead of the rich as the blessed of God, but it is good news they then have a responsibility to claim and inherit. There is a challenge in it for us all.

But there is a further honour being promised here to the poor for they have been challenged by Jesus not only to claim their heritage for the future, but to begin living it and experiencing that blessing right now. Some of the Beatitudes clearly point to the future – the hungry *shall* be fed; the sorrowful *shall* laugh; those who are hated *shall* be feted. But in the first Beatitude Jesus actually announces that the poor are blessed in the here and now – 'the Kingdom of God *is* yours'. The Pharisees believed that the Kingdom would only be realized if every Jew obeyed every detail of the Torah Law, but realists knew full well that the whole Jewish nation was unlikely to observe such a complex code of laws, and so the poor would always remain with them. The book of Deuteronomy therefore counselled (Deut. 15.11) that since this was the case all should live 'as if' the Kingdom had come and give generously.[5] But Jesus goes so far as to say that the Kingdom is actually breaking in right now, and we can glimpse signs of that Kingdom in our present experience – indeed, we have seen some of these signs among the poor already in our study, and we will be considering many more in due course. With Jesus we are no longer confined to acting only with the Deuteronomist 'as if' things might have been better, but we can live out the Kingdom now and yet know that there is also a future fulfilment of the Kingdom still to come – we live in the 'now and not yet' of the Kingdom. The opposition may look on and even appear to triumph, but we can live Kingdom lives now as a sign of what we know is already breaking into our story and will be perfected when the Kingdom is fully realized.

5 A good résumé of the history of this scholarship is to be found in Baker 2001. Even Jesus himself quoted the Deuteronomic proverb 'you have the poor with you always' (Mark 14.7), but in a very different context and certainly not to argue for the same restrictive conclusion.

Signs of the blessedness of the poor

We have taken time to listen to the voices of the poor, hearing their story and exploring the nature of their predicament. We have viewed all this through the gospel lens of the Lord's Prayer and looked afresh at Jesus' announcement about the special place the poor have in his plans. And all this has led us to talk of 'glimpses of the Kingdom' breaking through into the drab lives of poor people. The time has therefore now come to spell out precisely what some of these gifts and glimpses of Kingdom blessedness actually are. What are the proofs, if you will, that the poor are blessed?

Blessed by God's clear presence

It might appear for all the world that it is the rich and powerful who have God on their side – even Hitler was pleased to inscribe this claim, 'God With Us', on the belts of his soldiers. But Jesus makes it clear that it is otherwise. It was once popular for theologians to speak of God's 'option' or 'bias to the poor' (Sheppard 1983), but the Bible goes much further and announces that there is a positive discrimination towards them in the heart of God. It is writ large across the pages of the Hebrew Scriptures not only in the statements of the prophets, but in the poetry of the Psalms and in the story of a nation of slaves in Egypt who are given a very special place in God's history of redemption. This privileged place reaches its climax in the heart of the New Testament when Jesus lives alongside poor people to show them what the Kingdom is like, and to heal them with justice, mercy and forgiveness. We see here the poor blessed with a very special role in the redemption of the world and visited by a God whose justice is clearly partial towards them. It occurs to me that perhaps this after all is the reason why when I join the poor in worship in the draughty hall, there is a tangible sense that something special is going on. They are blessed by the very presence of God, as Jesus makes his home with them. And it is not only in worship that we experience this to be true. As a parish priest in a poor estate I was daily humbled to find the poor unwittingly instructing me in prayer, in pastoral care, in political acuity and simple warmth. And how often I came away from a home visit in silent tears not simply because of the stark deprivation in the home, but having sensed the palpable presence there of the God who really knows how to care and to be alongside.

Blessed by God's gifts

Iffi had been carefully led to the piano where he then mesmerized the audience by singing 'Amazing Grace' with passion and commitment. But it was when he reached the passage 'was blind but now I see' that our minds were wrenched to acknowledge the profound meaning that lay beyond the simplicity of the words. Jesus brings the marginalized to the centre and lets them teach us. Those who staff organizations that give the poor a platform so that their concerns and their perspectives can be heard are often deeply moved themselves and changed by the experience. It is as if they know themselves to be participating in the dynamic Jesus set in motion when he brought the child, the woman taken in adultery, the man with the withered hand and countless others to the centre of his circle and to the centre of his stories and miracles, and let them point us to yet more of the mysteries of the Kingdom. Those who care for the needy likewise reap a reward greater than ever they dispense, as any one of them will testify. Like Iffi, the marginalized seem gifted with an ability to teach others the deeper meanings, beyond the understandings we learn in the classroom. 'I've been teaching courses on jurisprudence for years,' said my lawyer friend, 'but only after sitting here with you this morning and listening to these people do I feel I now know the true meaning of justice – or perhaps I'd better say injustice!'

The third Beatitude tells the poor that laughter will be God's future blessing for them, but this blessing seeps in and spills over even in the present and can be seen in their ready wit and cheerfulness in the face of hardship. It can be quite disarming – 'well, you've got to laugh or you'd cry, wouldn't you!' Whenever I venture into the slums in India, I am always struck by the determination of the people to cover every surface with bright vivid colour wherever possible. And here among the UK's poor the same gift of celebration shines through the jokes, the fun language and the great parties. The TV soap writers never manage to do justice to this reality, and can only portray the anger. On visiting that group who were banding together to smarten up the young couple's home, even the pet rat seemed to have caught the mood of togetherness, the buzz of solidarity and the humour that was energizing the enterprise! The bring-and-share lunch at the estate church gathering seems always to elicit the quip 'it's like feeding the five thousand', and that humorous but profound insight suggests what fun that original gathering with Jesus must have been. When we are welcomed into one of these celebrations we know we are touching the deep culture of the people, whether they are serving curried goat and rice, jellied eels or chip butties. The fun of sharing food, dancing and joking, raises the spirit and rejoices even in adversity. The poor constantly seem blessed with the gift of rising to Paul's exhortation from his prison cell: 'Rejoice in the Lord always; again I will say, Rejoice' (Phil. 4.4, RSV).

Just sometimes we also have a glimpse of the Kingdom in the sense of gratitude we meet among the poor. It has a humbling quality that can bring us up short. In the night shelter most volunteers remark at one time or another how taken aback they are that those they are helping have thanked them for simply calling them by name. Of course, sometimes the poor can treat us as if we owe them a living – but, of course, we do! Perhaps to have the honesty to voice that is a gift too.

As well as gratitude, there is the blessedness of generosity. Many a Christian Aid collector, after going from door to door around the streets of the parish, will remark that they prefer to collect in poorer areas where they are likely to receive a warmer welcome and, comparatively speaking, a larger offering. It would seem that those who know hardship themselves are more open-minded about the needs of others, make fewer excuses not to give, and share what they have more generously. My own father would often use quite unsavoury language about his many Asian neighbours but was always the first to help if they were in trouble, and they in turn loved him and came out on to the streets to console my mother when he died. What's more, it often seems to be a very open-hearted giving which comes quite spontaneously to the poor, reminiscent of those in the story in Matthew's Gospel who asked, 'Lord, when did we see you hungry and feed you, or thirsty and give you drink? When did we see you a stranger and make you welcome, lacking clothes and clothe you?' (Matt. 25.37–38). Those who give in this unpremeditated way, says the parable, find themselves blessed indeed.

Blessed by faithfulness

It may sound odd at first, but the truth is that the poor are also blessed with the gift of faith. The Church likes to preach about faith, but sometimes has a rather obtuse notion of what it is. To wake up in the morning not knowing how one is to feed one's child, but nevertheless to face the day with determination and to struggle through to the end of it with a child fed and put to bed happy, is to live by faith indeed. But if the poor were not blessed by God with this gift, goodness knows how some would survive. The faithful parent may not put a name to the presence that gets them through each day, but there is no doubt that the faith is strong.

Two young mums had been living this hand-to-mouth existence in Hastings for 18 months when eventually the Seaview Centre managed to secure accommodation for them. A number of folk scouted round to rustle up some cooking implements and bedding and took it all round to them. The young girls – for young they were – took such delight in showing us round their tiny flat, the first they'd ever had. They knew they were totally dependent on the welfare of others, but the radiance with which they greeted their visitors was more than sufficient payment. One of the things the poor know is just how dependent on one another we truly are. The rich like to think of themselves as self-made, and we constantly hear political speeches deploring dependency – and this from people who have been educated by others, fed and served by others, and depend on others at every turn, as we all do. There is a right and wrong sort of dependency and the poor are blessed in knowing the importance of that distinction from harsh first-hand experience. That's why the main thing a poor person tries to read about you on a first meeting is whether you are dependable or not.

The greatest stimulus to prayer is awareness of our total dependence on God and that is why, when the Disciples ask Jesus how to pray (Luke 11.1), Luke records that he responds with a long lesson on how dependable God our loving Father is. He explains that even the shameless begging neighbour will receive eventually from his companion, and the boy who asks his father for a fish will not be given a snake (Luke 11.1–13). We should learn from the poor to own our dependency and become supplicants. The poor themselves are usually very wary of patronizing charity and want none of it, but do have an open hand to receive where there is generosity. Both the rich and the poor can of course grab – although the grabbing of the poor has at least some justice about it – but a readiness to own up to one's need and graciously accept the help of others is good training for receiving with open arms the love and generosity of God. Blessed are those who know how dependent they are on others and on a faithful God; it shows maturity and opens them to the gift of prayer, praise and gratitude.

The blessedness of vision

Because the poor are not cocooned from the harsh realities of life, as we've seen time and again, they really do see what is true and false about society in a way that no one else really can. Try as we may, those who are not poor or do not share their lives with the poor cannot truly comprehend the extent of the injustice that our society inflicts upon them. And unless we know the full measure of the suffering, we cannot fathom the immensity of God's sorrow and concern on hearing the sound of our brother's blood 'crying out to God from the ground' (Gen. 4.10). There is a blessedness, of course, simply in having a grasp on truth rather than living a life of illusion as most cocooned people do, but there is also the blessing of the anger that comes with knowing injustice for what it is. Without the energy that this anger generates there is little chance of injustice being addressed and properly attended to. A fully contented human being rarely helps change society for the better – but the poor certainly know it needs changing and can teach us to be angry too.

Of course, many of the poor are too confined by their poverty to play an active part in changing society, but many are still blessed with being change agents by virtue of their prophetic role, for they stand as a blessed warning to the rich and powerful. The rich cannot, says Jesus, be expected to get into the Kingdom of God (Matt. 19.24), just as the container truck has little chance of navigating its way through a keyhole nor the camel getting through the eye of a needle. So it is important that the rich are warned, if only by the simple presence of the poor, a warning that the rich Dives was only too keen to hear and share when it was all too late (Luke 16.19–31). Eileen and Rod make it their business to turn up at all the Community Forum meetings and are well-known to their local MP and councillors. They have sent pictures of unemptied dustbins and fouled stairwells to their local paper and attend rallies and protests when they can. They have to use their meagre incomes to do it, but they know that the poor are blessed with a prophetic role – they own that and fulfil it. As poor people they and many like them are well placed for this prophetic ministry, first because the poor do see where the inequalities and injustices lie because they are the ones who directly suffer from them, but also because they do not benefit as others do from the continuation of these injustices. All this is obvious when organizations set up 'urban hearings' in which the poor and the powerful are brought together to listen one to another. It can be an uncomfortable blessing for the powerful when they do the listening, because in many ways they have been cocooned from the realities of injustice, thinking that all is well when it is not. As they listen, that comfort is removed. In the past, they have heard only the poor being slagged off in the media and by their colleagues, but actually listening to the poor, however uncomfortable it may be, can save them from themselves. Listening to the poor is a blessing for us all.

The poor are often accused of having no sense of time, often late for appointments or rolling in late for church services. The reason for this may often be that they prefer to live in the present, since they have reason to forget the past, and the future is unstable and frightening. If money is available now, they spend it, because it is unlikely to be on offer tomorrow, and if they meet a friend, they might ignore the next appointment, because their vulnerable lives depend on friendships. On the other hand, the non-poor more usually miss the wonder of the present moment by swamping it with nostalgia for their past or concerns for their future career or investment. It may be infuriating that the poor pay scant attention to the future but, perhaps surprisingly, they can helpfully remind us to look out for the blessings of the present moment.

In the ancient Greek story the young shepherd boy Narcissus is so obsessed with himself that he has no time for those who love him. Eventually, while out hunting he stops by a pool and, lying down to drink, sees the reflection of his face in the water and falls in love with it. By the time his friends come looking for him, no person is left, only a drooping flower to bear his name. And to add to the tragedy, what he actually fell in love with was not even his real self but only a projected reflection in a pool. So much of human life is a projection, and often even our image of God can be only a projection of our own idealized self-image. The rich believe that the image of themselves that they project is actually worth their own devotion, but for all their bombast, poor people often have such a negative image of themselves that they do not aspire to project it on to God at all. It is a blessing for them that they are not so blinded by the haze of their own self-projections that they fail to see the glory of the true God.

The blessedness of vulnerability

In a way that is not open to the rich, the poor partake of a truth that is constantly repeated in the pages of the Bible: that the power of God is revealed in what we perceive to be weakness. The Hebrew Scriptures are replete with examples of God choosing the most unlikely to be the instrument of the people's destiny. Isaac is born to Sarah when she was past the age of child-bearing; David is anointed as king from among the shepherds; and Mary, a single girl in a backwater town, is chosen to give birth to the saviour of the world. Paul in his letters speaks of how 'God chose what is weak in the world to shame the strong, God chose what is low and despised in the world, even things that are not, to bring to nothing things that are, so that no human being might boast in the presence of God' (1 Cor. 1.27–29). When God shines through the weak, it saves us all from boasting of our own strength. And it is this vulnerability, after all, this openness to risk, that is the prerequisite of true love. To love demands that we lower our defences and reveal to our beloved our true self with all our faults and weaknesses, and in this way we lay ourselves open to the risk of being hurt by the one we love most. Many having been hurt in this way find it hard to be vulnerable and to love again, and that is the biggest risk of all. But the poor are well-versed in living with constant vulnerability, and that does allow God's love to enter in and make a home more readily in their heart.

It is for this reason that some non-poor people, seeking to make themselves open to God's love, have intentionally made themselves vulnerable by choosing to live a life of poverty themselves. Many have entered monastic communities, giving all their possessions away so that, as Sister Mary John tells me, they may 'not be possessed by anything but God'. This attempt to empty the self of oneself in order that God can fill that empty space was seen by many of the earliest teachers of the Church to be the best way of following the example of Jesus' actions on the cross – what they termed *kenosis* or self-emptying. Francis of Assisi, the brother of the poor, came so close to the cross in his poverty that he even found the marks of the nails, the stigmata, appearing on his hands. Thomas Aquinas too saw a very clear link, as Christopher Franks explains, between loving vulnerability, the cross, and poverty, by emphasizing that: 'From first to last, a humble vulnerability echoing Christ on the cross conditions Christian economic action' (Franks 2009, p. 107). This profound sense of lowliness before God, which remains the goal of those who seek to emulate the vulnerability of the poor by voluntarily joining them in their poverty, opens them to many of the blessings that we have begun to enumerate. They make themselves weak so that God's power may abound.

But the Benedictine nuns that have guided me are quick to point out some dangers too. First, Aquinas ran the great risk of giving the impression that since poverty was the royal road to holiness, poverty itself should be hallowed, which certainly is not what Jesus taught. This was why Benedict never asked his followers to take a vow of poverty, and to this day they submit instead to a vow of 'conversion of life', which of course includes living very simply indeed and sharing everything, but never allows poverty to be seen as holy in itself. I have myself heard it said that the poor are blessed because they do not have to worry about possessions as the rich have to, and while there may well be some slight truth in this, how patronizing it sounds when uttered by someone who has the security of much wealth! Many a poor person would gladly swap their cold flat for a mansion, to save the wealthy worrying about their stocks and shares. So we must remember that calling the poor blessed only makes sense in the wider context of fighting for Kingdom justice and the eradication of poverty – without working for this radical justice as Jesus does, no one can ever with integrity call the poor blessed. It is this very careful Kingdom balance of commending and emulating the blessedness of the poor while simultaneously working for radical justice in the world that might best be summed up in the words that Matthew chooses to frame the Beatitude – 'Blessed are the poor in spirit'. We learned earlier in this chapter that Matthew's Jewish readers would have been reminded by his careful wording of the many insights that the Hebrew words for the poor carried with them, together with an awareness of the Jubilee expectation of the restoration of equality in the land. So the poor in spirit are the ones who vulnerably empty themselves of the clutter of self while working to see God's Kingdom of justice established in our society – as he draws out by adding 'blessed are those who hunger and thirst for righteousness . . . Blessed are the peacemakers, for they shall be called sons of God' (Matt. 5.6–9, RSV). So it is those who try to be alongside the poor, voluntarily making themselves one with the poor, while at the same time fighting with them for justice and an equal sharing of God's good gifts, who also thereby find themselves very close to Jesus who emptied himself so completely on the cross – they are the poor in spirit.

Christians speak of 'thin places', where the distance between us and the Divine is reduced to a sliver. The sacrament of Holy Communion is such a place, and just as he promises to be present to us in that holy sacrament, so too he promises his real presence with us in the poor when he says: 'in so far as you did this to one of the least of these brothers of mine, you did it to me' (Matt. 25.40). To be among the poor we are in an extraordinarily thin place for here we are with those he christens 'the blessed', and by calling them that he gives them his seal of approval. Jesus himself receives a similar seal of approval when at his baptism God says: 'This is my Son, the Beloved; my favour rests on him' (Matt. 3.17). The Beatitudes then in turn set his seal of approval upon the poor, making them his very closest brothers and sisters in the Kingdom, helping to lead the Church forward as the vanguard of his Kingdom promise.

7

Blessed with Insight

Pope Francis has been forthright in his plea to the Church that we do not simply view poor people as those for whom we should care, but that we ask them to take centre stage and help the Church find its Kingdom bearings and change its lifestyle to become a 'Church that is poor and for the poor. They have much to teach us' (Pope Francis 2013, §198). He is right to point out that the Church has been far too inclined to interpret matters from the perspective of those who have prestige and power in society and who live lives that are cocooned from the vagaries and vulnerabilities which are the everyday fare of the poor. But Christianity originated amid those very insecurities, and when the poor help the Church to look again at the texts and treasures of our faith from the perspective of that vulnerability, then new light dawns, and we see again some of their original, challenging meanings.

The poor's blessings of biblical insight

Greg was very new to church, and this was his first visit to a Bible study meeting. We were looking at such a well-known passage that I had anticipated that we would simply rehearse ideas that we'd all heard many times before. Everyone had heard that the story of the widow's mite (Mark 12.41–44) was intended to encourage us to be more generous givers, but Greg had never heard the usual interpretation before, so he came at the story afresh, informed only by his own life-experience. 'We've just read that Jesus was having a go at the bosses right? The scribes and those people? And now he's in the bank-place, and they're screwing her for every penny she's got. And he doesn't like it. It's really up-to-date stuff this!' Greg had quite rightly realized from attention to the context that this story comes as the culmination of two chapters of heady conflict between Jesus and the authorities, and it also acts as the introduction to Jesus' prediction of the destruction of the Temple and the coming of the Son of man. In the middle of this horrendous conflictual discourse was it likely that Mark would interject a story about how nice it is to give to charity? Surely, this story was placed here to alert us to how even religious institutions are not averse to inflicting oppressive injustice upon the poorest of the poor. Greg had spotted this intuitively, but only years later have alert biblical scholars realized that Greg was absolutely right (Myers 1998, pp. 320–3).

There has grown up through the years a disagreement about what controlling principles should govern our interpretation of biblical texts. For many generations, scholars followed an approach proposed by Augustine of Hippo and others in the fourth and fifth centuries. Their Graeco-Roman minds assumed that a society was like a human body in that it was 'natural' that each societal group or bodily organ acted in harmony with the next. If one element was for some reason out of harmony with the rest, they deduced that the offending organ was acting 'against nature' and would have to be subdued for the sake of the whole body or society. The maintenance of order and harmony was paramount. This understanding was welcomed by the powers that be, because it gave them warrant to keep oppositional forces silent, even if on occasion those forces had justice on their side. So Greg had brought to our attention a fine example of the way the story of the widow's mite has through the years been subjected to just such an interpretation – for despite the fact that it is primarily an attack on the injustices perpetrated by the authorities of the day, it has been interpreted as an encourager for even the poorest folk to pay their dues to those authorities and maintain 'order'. We can call this approach a 'hermeneutic of order', the word 'hermeneutic' being the scholar's word for any approach we take to the interpretation of a text or a situation. So a hermeneutic of order interprets anything by starting from the principle that the maintenance of order is fundamental to truth. The liberation theologian José Míguez Bonino in his book *Toward a Christian Political Ethics* has suggested a different approach altogether, which he calls a 'hermeneutic of justice' – one that adopts the perspective of the poor and, as the name implies, looks to the principle of justice as the key to biblical interpretation. As Bonino puts it, 'The true question is not "What degree of justice (liberation of the poor) is compatible with the maintenance of the existing order?" but "*What kind of order is compatible with the exercise of justice (the right of the poor)*?"' (Bonino 1983, p. 86). For him, it is justice rather than order that is more true to the values of the Kingdom and therefore should be our guiding principle as we interpret biblical texts – and as we have already seen, because the poor in our society are best placed to discern where the injustices are, their insights will be crucial to any interpretation according to this hermeneutic of justice. They will not be approaching the text from the perspective of the powerful, the Temple authorities and the scribes, but from that of the slaves in Egypt, the exiles in Babylon, the crucified poor of the Roman Empire and the labourers in the vineyard. What's more, they will be looking for insights that make sense in their own lives as poor people – insights that speak of the need for togetherness, justice and practical action, rather than philosophical speculation and the merits of the status quo.

I want to demonstrate how this works in practice by offering a few illustrations of how the experiences and perspective of poor people can bring new insights to the fore. For example, I recently sat in the café at the British Library discussing these matters with an old friend, Anthony Harvey, who having written extensively on the New Testament and about Jesus' teaching (1990, 2004) had offered to help me with my research. I happened to mention that I had never before appreciated that the word 'exclusion' appears in Luke's version of the Beatitudes. He looked quizzically at me and admitted: 'I can't now remember exactly where that word appears in the text.' We scrabbled in the Greek New Testament, and there it was, in verse 22. Anthony's eyes lit up with excitement as he translated – 'blessed are you when people hate you, drive you out'. He then proceeded to offer a wealth of historical background and scholarship that suddenly made sense to me of what it must have been like for Jesus' contemporaries when they heard that fourth Beatitude for the first time. Jesus was alluding to the way that being poor shuts you out from the rest of society. For example, those first Jewish listeners would have been aware, said Anthony, that being shut out from the synagogue would have annulled the security that synagogue registration conferred upon them as Jews in the Roman Empire – it was very dangerous to find oneself excluded! But why hadn't either of us noticed the word 'exclusion' there before? I dare to suggest it was because neither of us had personal experience of the inextricable link between poverty and exclusion, so it had not triggered our keenest interest until we assumed a hermeneutic of justice. On another occasion, I was taking part in a Bible study on Mark 1.29–31, the story of the healing by Jesus of Simon Peter's mother-in-law. In the group were two African asylum-seekers who, when we reached verse 31, were thrilled with delight and exclaimed, 'Well, that could never happen where we come from!' The verse simply said that the fever left Peter's mother-in-law, and she served them food. These two women were struck by the fact that although she was a woman who had been ill recently, she was not now considered unclean and excluded, and was immediately allowed by Jesus to touch the food that would serve the company. That inclusion was for those two excluded asylum-seekers the answer to their daily prayer. But I had never noticed how important it was in the text before.

Once we place ourselves alongside the experience of poor people and adopt this hermeneutic of justice, we will be able to read the text in these new ways almost at every turn. For example, the poor know that solidarity is crucial for survival when the pressure is on. How inadequate therefore to translate the Greek word *koinonia* as 'fellowship' – which would not have sustained the early Christians through their years of persecution. The hermeneutic of order has been content to translate the word in that rather limp way, but a hermeneutic of justice will call it 'solidarity'.

In like manner, being alongside poor people can also offer us new ways into understanding the sufferings and joys of Jesus. The court-room's prejudiced travesties that surrounded him before his crucifixion readily resonate with their own experiences at the hands of the authorities – where they are easily misunderstood and feel things are stacked against them.

Again, I have been to many a cockney party where inside the flat all is singing, dancing and fun, but in the kitchen or on the doorstep with the smokers the problems and the sorrows of their daily life are talked through and intimately shared – after which some will return to the celebration, and others will come out to pick up the thoughtful conversation, until they too feel it's time for them to join the party once more. It's an interesting dynamic, which naturally allows the interconnectedness of struggle and celebration to be lived out. The poor know that you cannot really have the joys of resurrection without the sorrows of Good Friday. For all the exhilaration of Easter morning, the heartache of the cross must still be owned.

Exclusion and exile

As we've mentioned, the biblical theme of exclusion speaks loud and clear to many people in poverty today, and they bring new insights to those Bible passages that allude to it. The word that Anthony Harvey and I struggled with over coffee in the British Library was *aphorizein*, which appears within the fourth Beatitude to mean, literally 'to separate you off'. Jesus addresses the poor and says, you will be blessed when 'people hate you, separate you off, abuse you, denounce your name as criminal, on account of the Son of man' (our paraphrasing, Luke 6.22). As Anthony explained, in the medieval period the fear was of exclusion from Paradise, as the doom murals in ancient churches signify, but today poor people have to deal with a vast range of exclusions that are quite alarming. If they live in certain areas, they will not be trusted by prospective employers, banks or credit agencies or might be excluded from good education, proper health care and access to services. Lack of money precludes you from better shopping facilities, decent communication media, travel and home heating. The poor are residualized into the poorest estates and, to cap it all, are ostracized by shame – I well remember how even our own vicarage children were mocked in the playground for not being able to afford fashionable trainers.

The Jewish exile into Babylon casts a long shadow across the pages of the Hebrew Scriptures and in so many ways resonates even today with the experiences of people on poor estates. Once the exiled Jews had lived at the crossroads of the world, situated on the great trade route between the civilizations of Egypt and Assyria, but in the sixth century BC Israel was crushed by the mighty Babylonian Empire. A large proportion of the population were ripped out from all they had known and made to settle on foreign soil amid an alien culture. On reaching the place of exile, they received a letter from the prophet Jeremiah which is reproduced in the Bible, and many estate congregations have studied it with interest. Jeremiah writes that he senses God saying to them: '. . . settle down; plant gardens and eat what they produce; marry and have sons and daughters . . . Work for the good of the city to which I have exiled you; pray to Yahweh on its behalf, since on its welfare yours depends' (Jer. 29.5–7). Poor estate tenants know how it is when, like those exiles, they feel everything is against them. It is so easy to opt for crime, fall into apathy, or even to riot. But the Jeremiah option is the way of no ducking out, always seeking to rise above despair despite being cognizant of the grim realities. The Babylonian exiles found it hard to sing their songs of praise in this alien land and at times sat down and wept (Ps. 137.4). But they also composed songs and poems of lament and righteous anger at the injustice around them, and these songs resonate even now in our estate churches: 'How long, O LORD? Will you forget me for ever? How long will you hide your face from me? How long must I bear pain in my soul, and have sorrow in my heart all day long?' (Ps. 13.1–2, NRSV). These laments did not seek to evade the realities of the exile; they did not sound a romantic or jingoistic note but simply spoke of trust in God amid the horror of it all. 'I trusted in your steadfast love . . . I will sing to the LORD' (v. 5, NRSV). And it is perhaps this trust against all the odds that I have sensed during my worship on the poor estates. Continuing to keep things together as a congregation week after week and year after year is a minor miracle in itself and speaks volumes about their depth of faith despite the ongoing offensiveness of exclusion.

Exile and exclusion make you feel you are forgotten – forgotten by the state, by the Church, and perhaps even by God. The youngsters I had spoken with on the street were clear that they were forgotten and of no concern to the wider society unless they raised havoc – and perhaps that is why they liked to do just that. It is a natural instinct when forgotten to scream out to make people notice. I asked Roscoe if he believed in God, and he answered: 'Sure I do, but he doesn't care about us, does he. He's forgotten we're here.' Jeremiah's letter was sent to remind the exiles that God did care and had not forgotten them. That is why when Jesus is born he is given the name Emmanuel, which means 'God is with us' – never forgetting us but with us in every exile and every excluded housing estate. When Jesus tells his poor disciples to 'do this *in remembrance* of me' (1 Cor. 11.24–25), he makes his Church into a community that never forgets and is never forgotten.

Nehemiah

The hermeneutic of justice also provides the poor with an intriguing new insight into the book of Nehemiah – the autobiography of that great figure who at the end of the exile helps bring the Jews back to rebuild the city of Jerusalem. Usually Nehemiah is hailed as the great hero of the re-establishment of the nation of Israel, but the poor have another take on this character, which is far from flattering. Nehemiah likes to picture himself as a man of some consequence in the court of the Persian King and tells us how he manages to convince the palace to bank-roll the regeneration of Jerusalem. This privileged and wealthy exile returns to find that the truly forgotten poor, who were so deprived that the Babylonians had not even bothered to exile them, had managed to survive nevertheless and were still in what was left of the old city and its environs. These left-behind folk had, however, intermarried with the locals, whom Nehemiah and his returning exiles consider impure, and so Nehemiah accuses them of having bastardized the purity of their Jewish bloodline. They have become known as the Samaritans and as the Poor of the Land (Rubenstein 2003, p. 124). Nehemiah therefore deals very harshly with them (chapter 4), refusing their offers of help, moving forward with his secretive building plans (Neh. 2.12) and clearing them out of the locality. This is reminiscent of when the London Olympic Park was being built among the poor estates of the East End. The local rents were driven sky high, forcing many of the poor to move out. The thrill of the Olympic Games was never forgotten, but the local poor were.

It's also alarming to see that later when Nehemiah's strategy seems to be failing, he returns to the city and blames the foreign women whom the locals have married, literally tearing their hair out in a ferocious, racist attack (chapter 13). Racism is never far from the surface where delusions about one's own purity are in the air and when the powerful wish to divert attention from their own culpabilities. But despite all this horror the city of Jerusalem is rebuilt and stands as a testimony to Nehemiah's life. He ends his somewhat biased memoirs with the words: 'Remember this, my God, to my credit!' (Neh. 13.31, RSV). These questionable aspects of the story are usually glossed over or not even recognized by those who adopt a hermeneutic of order, but the poor have been on the receiving end of this type of regeneration policy so often that they know to their cost what it is to have no trustworthy representation, made compulsorily homeless, pushed aside to allow others in and even blamed for any public failures that may come to the surface later. 'This story really helps me when I see it this way,' said Maria. 'I can understand better how I feel here in London, but it also makes me think about what's happening to my family who are still in Ramallah.'

Nehemiah's top-down mission is totally at odds with that of Jesus who instead lives among the impure People of the Land throughout his life and is even accused of being a Samaritan himself (John 8.48)! He gathers the poor around him to share with them his insights and his programme for change – an inclusive programme that empowers from below and seeks out the spark of the Spirit of God within even the most unlikely of the poor, including the Samaritan. These two contradictory styles of mission – the indigenous approach of Jesus and the invasive practices of Nehemiah – will be instructive for us when later we discuss the missiological practice appropriate to Kingdom living.

Understanding the importance of place

We only have room to mention one more example of how the gifts of the poor open up our understandings of Scripture and assist Christians in living according to Kingdom values. Early in our study we were reminded of the importance of history in the Hebrew Scriptures in helping the Jewish people discern the hand of God upon them, and this encouraged us to look at the history – the story – of the poor housing estates. But while history concerns itself with the story through time, the other great theme of the Hebrew Scriptures is the story of the sacred place – the Promised Land. And the two, time and place, are bound together in those Scriptures, in that the history of Judaism is seen to revolve around God's gift of the Promised Land to his people; how they must care for it and share its bounty in accordance with the Torah ordinances. The poor today are similarly aware of the importance of the place they inhabit, how it can make them feel they belong, and how damaging it is to the spirit when they feel alienated from it. Older members of the community may never have strayed from the estate more than once or twice in their whole lives, while hardened youngsters will claim the local streets as their turf. While others may understand their lives increasingly as zonal, mobile and networked, the poor remain more concrete in the ways they like to belong. Relationships are largely street-based and family and locality-centred,[1] and even estate youngsters who live on their mobile phones are not as mobile as the gadgets imply. Like others, they may be in touch with chat-rooms around the globe, but their roots remain on the local streets where they hang out together on particular corners

1 See, for example, Hasler 2006.

or in the tatty shopping precincts. Edward Soja, the postmodern geographer and urban planner, has been very keen to remind us that we all in fact live in concrete and not abstract places (2010). We transform the land on which we walk by turning these hollow spaces into treasured places by investing each location with stories, memories and special associations. The poor are adept at walking the urban streets and 'reading' a place as a crucible of stories and power relations, if only for the purposes of self-preservation and to establish their own identity within the space. I have found that this facility helps them perceive the symbolism of the places in the Bible too. 'Life's like that,' said Trace, 'you're going along fine then everything goes pear-shaped and blows up in your face. That's what that Sea of Galilee is like – OK most of the time, and then all hell breaks loose. If Jesus comes walking over that without falling in, I'd love to know how he does it 'cos I can't. I just stay indoors and keep my head down.' Gavin interjected – 'But he does better than that; he calms it all down so the fellas can get back to work. That's what we need round here.'

Each place also has its distinctive sounds and the poor are therefore instinctively alert to the meaning of local accents – even the differences from estate to estate. Peter is sitting in the courtyard of the palace where Jesus is being interrogated by the Sanhedrin, when he is accosted by a bystander who assumes by his strange northern accent that he must therefore be a trouble-maker and a friend of Jesus the northern misfit (Matt. 26.74). Nathaniel was similarly concerned that Jesus had northern roots, when he questioned whether anything good could come out of Nazareth (John 1.46). I saw a Scripture Union cartoon video in a school assembly recently, in which all the Disciples spoke with northern accents. I was fascinated that the teachers were disconcerted about these 'uncouth' accents – quite unfitting for followers of Jesus they felt, even in a cartoon video. Not only the postcode, but the sound of a place can ruin your chances of a future. Perhaps this is why the poor's appreciation of context is more acute than most, not only when reading the street but also reading the Bible.

Our meditation on the Lord's Prayer taught us how the 'down-to-earth' incarnation of Jesus committed him to a specific context of place and time and how he honoured that rather than deny it, never choosing to speak or teach in vague abstractions. The backdrop against which all his parables are set is very local, and even after the resurrection he is pleased to return to his native Galilee where he evidently feels at home. The poor help us to have eyes that are contextually astute when we turn to the study of Scripture and when we move out into mission. They remind us that God made space for us.

Theological insights of the poor

I trust that the few examples we have offered serve to give a flavour of how the experience of poor people allows for a fresh appreciation of the people and stories of the Bible in all sorts of new ways. We see the biblical characters come alive, the situations become ever more significant, and the lessons we draw go straight to the heart of the matter. We see things that had previously escaped our notice, and we receive new insights into those stories we thought we already understood. And most challenging of all, these new insights invariably point us to Kingdom values and provoke us to think again about the part we play in the subtle workings of injustice.

But the biblical texts are not the only treasures in which the Church glories. We have inherited a whole world of treasures – the holy sacraments, our Christian music, art and ecclesiology, theological ideas and discoveries in the realms of science, sociology, philosophy and politics. And just as with the biblical text, so with each of these spheres of Christian experience when we approach them from the perspective of the poor; once again new light dawns, new sensitivities emerge, and fresh commitments are made. How does this happen?

As recently as 20 years ago, there would have been a strong deposit of residual Christian belief among Britain's poor, but surveys indicate that that is no longer the case. A large proportion of children today when asked who Jesus is, guess that he might be a footballer, or believe that at Christmas we remember the birth of

Elvis or lately the Christmas penguin. It's a sorry state of affairs. The last generation to carry memories of the Bible stories has now moved into late retirement and will soon no longer be with us. Only families newly arrived from Africa or from Catholic countries will probably still carry these traditions. But although this religious 'content' is fast vanishing, the poor have given us an even more valuable theological treasure to assist us – a theological method.

The poor's method began not from asking the academic's question: 'How can we believe in a God in a world of science?' but from the poor's question: 'How can we believe in a personal God in a world which denies our personhood?' (McAfee Brown 1979, p. viii). And while old-fashioned theological reflection spoke at length about its social concern, the poor were framing a theological method that set about actually doing something about those concerns. In Latin America, small groups of poor people, known as base communities, developed a method that started by looking at their own situation, and from that context discerned truths about God, the Bible, and the possibility of their own liberation from oppression. Similar things were developing in the USA among the Black community and here in the UK among women and the poor, and my own contribution was to express the new method in a diagrammatic form, adapting a cyclic diagram I had picked up from adult learning theory.[2] So although the descriptive commentaries and the circular diagram did not come directly from the poor, the method itself most certainly did. And today we thank the poor for that which we now call 'contextual theology' as we bring that methodology to bear upon those other Christian treasures.

Christological insights

Christology is that area of theology that concentrates on trying to understand the nature of the God–man, Jesus Christ. And it's here

2 For the history of the development of contextual theology in the UK, see Green 2013 and Green 2009, p. 17.

that the poor immediately encounter a problem. For as soon as the Church began to be led by the more powerful members of society, it purposefully stressed the heavenly and ethereal nature of Christ as one to be worshipped in his majesty and otherness, and they attacked as heretics those they felt were over-emphasizing the role of the down-to-earth Jesus. We can still see evidence of this in the Church's creeds which go on at length about the Son's heavenly relationship with the Father, with ne'er a word about Jesus' teaching, healing and life with the poor. The nearest the Church and its creeds came to recognizing the Jesus of the poor was to teach them that he was the crucified Suffering Servant foretold by Isaiah as the man of sorrows, acquainted with grief (Isa. 53), and it instructed them to emulate the tearful Virgin Mary and the accepting Jesus of Gethsemane, while relegating the text of Mary's revolutionary song (Luke 1.46–55) to polite Cathedral plainchant, so that they never heard that 'the mighty will be put down from their thrones'. According to this model, Jesus became the poor ascetic who demonstrated that poverty is holy and who taught us to keep our minds away from material concerns and directed towards heaven.

All this is a very long way from the man Jesus we have been meeting as we have listened to the experiences of the poor. I asked Rod about him. 'Well, he's the main man, isn't he? He does all those miracles and things and that's pretty cool. Only one man's been able to do that.' Being a main man is not to say that he is automatically followed, but it certainly means that he is not to be insulted and is to be regarded as a model for others. The slogan 'What would Jesus do?' makes a lot of sense to poor people, and many poor Christians have taken that as their motto for life. Rod also talked of Jesus as 'the best teacher ever', imparting truth not in a pedantic way but in a way he could appreciate and admire. The difficulty in talking of Jesus as teacher is, however, that for many poor people teachers are seen as judgemental, Christianity itself being thought of in that way – as merely a judgemental ethical standard: 'Oh, I'm a Christian: I hate swearing and all that.' But Rod was quick to mention his sports teacher, who would take team members in his own car to matches, and there was the kindly woman teacher, who would take time to chat with the girls about their worries and ease their sobbing. So there is also for some a very strong sense that Jesus himself, while being very special and holy, is paradoxically also their best mate or their hidden intimate – someone to spend time with, dependable and willing to listen. In this, there is something of the Street Mother about him – the person you pop round to see, who sorts things out for you, solves your problems and cuddles you when it's all too much. But Street Mothers have their own lives to lead too and do sometimes tell you 'to get on with it and stand on your own feet'. Sometimes Jesus can be difficult like that.

Knowing Jesus as an authoritative and demanding teacher who is also profoundly intimate and caring is to know a Jesus who models a radical egalitarianism where the master is also the servant, where the first make themselves last so that the last can be first, where privilege and distinction are spurned and the ground levelled. Jesus makes himself a nobody so that all may know that in God's company they are all somebody. Through his own radical engagement this is a Jesus who levels society and gives us all access to the Father, regardless of our status.[3] This was an understanding that the powerful medieval Church found very challenging – so challenging in fact that they considered it verging on the heretical since it endangered their power and privilege.

But this human Jesus is the one the poor get excited about, and not only because of his earthy, street-wise reality, but because they sense that this is the way to encounter the Holy – and they are much more interested in meeting than they are in just hearing about God. When I've asked estate church members what parts of the service are most dear to them, most answer that it's when walking up to receive Communion – that moment when Jesus seems to draw most near to them, entering into their very bodies in the bread, in the most earthy and intimate way possible. And this bread is proclaimed as the Body of Christ, that Jesus who is their best mate, down to earth and yet of heaven too, local and yet mysteriously other. It is 'Holy Communion' – the moment the

3 Compare John Dominic Crossan, 1992, Part II, 'Brokerless Kingdom'.

holy is made common among them, and the common people of the estate are made holy.

The poor help us see that the Christological question is not so much to do with the conundrum of how Jesus can be human and divine simultaneously – the poor live with hybridity all the time – but about how Jesus' relationship with God makes us a somebody by making himself a nobody, like us. For a poor person this really is good news! Jesus is the one who introduces us to a God who demands that we think again about who we are because of who he is. Meeting Jesus is to realize that the difficult kid at the back of the class, the father who beats his children, the mother who sits in front of the TV all day and forgets the children, can all now be seen again for what they really are – fallen yes, like all human beings, but carrying within themselves the spark of the holy, the spirit of the resurrection waiting to be fanned into flame. And all this because of who Jesus the man really is – divine made human that each human person may find again the image of the Divine within.

T-shirts and thin places

A very scholarly bishop friend had asked to come to see the parish, and we had a wonderful time together, but as we walked the streets I became aware that he was tripping over things on the pavement, was unable to read the traffic, or to sense who you could talk to on the street and who was best steered clear of. He kept telling me that we needed a synoptic vision of the urban, which sounded all very fascinating I'm sure, but he was thoroughly inept when it came to seeing where he was. The estate poor are brought up to be very street literate – they not only read, but they write too, displaying intriguing slogans on their T-shirts and on the graffitied walls. The theatre of surfaces is played out at every moment (Raban 1974) in the meaning of the tattoos, the angle of the hat, or the grunt of disapproval. Signs of belonging, distance, identity and criticism are written everywhere for those who have eyes to read them. In 'The Body: Physicality in the UPA'

(Green 1995, pp. 105ff.), I describe how their physical presence and even the non-verbal communication of body language is the natural environment of the poor, leading their reader into deeper meanings and nuances wherever they look or listen. Their whole place is alive with sacraments of meaning.

The sacraments of the Church are those thin places where we meet God deep within the physical – the bread and wine of Communion, the water of baptism, the oil of healing, the Salvation Army's flag of salvation, the teddy bear on the cemetery flagstone. Those who are spiritually sensitive have a way of discerning those thin places – those situations in which we find the distance between ourselves and our God wafer-thin. 'Having the baby done' may not pass the Church's orthodoxy test, but it puts mum and baby in touch with matters that touch us at night, when we are alone with our innermost thoughts, but we would never dare mention on the tough-talking streets. And the party afterwards is not just to have a good time, but a chance for the baby and parents to be brought to the centre of attention for once in their life, in just the way Jesus always did with the poor. That's why the word 'Christening' has coinage among the poor, when the word 'baptism', which literally only means dipping, quite frankly does not. The word 'Christen', after all, has the same punch of identity as the name 'Christ'. 'When we all line up at the pearly gates', said Andy, 'Jesus Christ will dart out and pull us out of the line and say "this one's mine".'

When we see God in a little wafer of bread, we are 'getting our eye in', so that we can see the Divine more clearly in other things through the week. For it is the God in the small things of life who most readily appeals to the poor of the estates. Making tea for friends, popping round to check old Donald next door, turning up at the boring church meeting on a cold night, these are the little signs of commitment that might not seem much to others but are our sacraments to God. It's as if these sacraments are not so much God talking to us as us talking to God, for God is sign-literate too – we discover among the poor, in their culture of physicality, just how much sacraments are a two-way communication. As well as being God's communication to us, they are also the way that the God of the poor listens to our little tweets of daily worship – our prayer without ceasing.

Traditional sacramental theology draws our attention to a very important matter. During the liturgy of the Communion the priest looks to heaven and asks that God will come down upon the bread and the wine and make it special through the indwelling of the Holy Spirit. This moment is called the *epiclesis*, or invocation of the Spirit. This doctrine alerts us to the fact that while some things and places are certainly thinner places than others, it is still up to God to make them so. A similar thing must happen when the Church moves into mission. If mission is our action alone, and we have not even bothered to ask God to be present in it, then it will be doomed to insignificance – it will not be significant of God's action. So when a church undertakes a project in the community, it must likewise be sure to ask God to make that project a thin place. This will become clear when we talk about mission and ministry, but suffice it here to say that, for example, when any project or programme is set up by a Christian community, it has the possibility of becoming sacramental if, and only if, there is woven into its very fabric ongoing prayer and the opportunity for theological reflection upon it at the moment of its conception, during its development, throughout its life, and there again at its end. The praxis of action/reflection, upon which the cycle of doing contextual theology is based, depends entirely upon this waiting upon God at every moment, so that all our actions can become sacramental signs – so that we see the deeply significant meaning that God plants within them. If our projects are not sacramental in this sense, then we should not undertake them. But if they are, they become acted parables, sacraments of the Kingdom. Our projects become significant – they signify.

Power and the Church

'It doesn't help much that Jesus said do to others what you want them to do to you, father, because all we get is people doing things to us. When did we last get a chance to do anything to them?'

In matters of importance to their lives, like housing, schooling, travel or welfare benefits, the poor have little choice, because others make the decisions about their lives. It begs the question, if God wants society changed, why is God's Messiah incarnated among people who are powerless? When Pope Francis writes that he wants the Church to be a Church of the poor, many ask the same question – how can locating the Church among the powerless lead to any progress in a world where power is what matters?

Power sometimes issues from those who for all the world do not appear to be powerful at all, and it is not at all a power that is assumed or taken for granted by them. 'All these advertising logos – but just compare them with the cross! It's just a picture of Jesus dying, but it's got more power than all of them put together. It makes you stop and think – they don't!' Jack was poor and had little to no economic clout, but he was able to read visual signs very well. He was a man of bold humility, powerless – and yet with a courageous power that his very humility gave him. We expect to find power only in violence, money or political leverage, but certain individuals demonstrate extraordinary power from a position of powerlessness. Nelson Mandela was known by his fellow prisoners on Robbin Island as 'the Smile', which we're told was extraordinarily disarming of the powers around him.

In the past the Church, however, has often delighted in expecting the privilege of power, assuming that it will be given a seat at the top table. How this contrasts with the humility of the resurrected Jesus, who enters and sits at the table in Emmaus only after he has been pressed to take his place by his travelling companions (Luke 24.28). A famous picture has him waiting patiently at the door, knocking. There is an astounding modesty here which to a power-hungry world makes little sense. Again, the picture of the Trinity in the famous icon created by the Russian monk Rublev shows three visitors who have been welcomed in. They are gathered around a central table to eat a humble meal together. Their red staffs, an iconic symbol of power, are all of exactly the same length, and even though one is in the centre, there is strangely no feeling when looking at the picture of any one of the figures being of more importance than the others. There is an intimacy of sharing in their faces and posture, and a wide space is left in front for the viewer to take their place round the table, ushered forward by the body language of the figure on the right representing the Holy Spirit, so that the circle may be complete. The figures ooze power, and at the same time they display a serene gentleness, harmony and an air of deference one to the other. This icon portrays how power is shared within the Holy Trinity – a power altogether different from the worldly power we know so well. We can see the solidarity of the three – the need that each has of the other, the respect each has for the other and the calm sense of self and personhood that each receives from that mutual affirmation. Here we see represented 'power for' and not 'power over'.

But time and again Christians get this all wrong, assuming that we should present a picture of ourselves as powerful, carrying a mandate to take biblical truth and bludgeon others with it. We have parachuted ourselves into areas with our message of salvation without thinking to ask where God is already present with those upon whom we descend. But of late society has been less prepared to give religion access to power and has begun not only to criticize it but to ridicule and marginalize it. Paradoxically, however, this may be just what we need, since it will put us back where we belong, with others who are powerless and marginalized, and give us the emotional energy to act as critic of the powers and not their chaplain. To help us remember this we can look to one of the symbols of this type of servanthood in the Church – the deacon. When someone is first ordained, they are made a deacon – which simply means a 'servant'. They assist the people – and especially the priest – in many of the Church's tasks, not least the services. But only after the deacon has fully understood and really inhabited that role as a servant are they then allowed to be ordained priest – for the Church has always taught that if a priest who has certain powers within the Church ever forgets that the heartwood of their vocation is that of servant, they are doomed – and so probably is the Church they serve!

But the poor remind us that there can even be a problem about servanthood, for it is easy to adopt a servant mentality that is not in accordance with Kingdom values. Our servanthood should be modelled on that of Jesus, who empowered the lowly and critiqued the powerful, but the poor have been downtrodden for so long that some have learned to survive by adopting instead a victim mentality. Many women in abusive relationships have shared with me the horror of being in this powerless position and yet finding it difficult to liberate themselves from playing out the role of the martyr – power can be this destructive of persons. The Church has concentrated for too long on teaching the poor to be servile, the Book of Common Prayer even teaching us to say: 'there is no health in us . . . miserable offenders'. A proper understanding of the servanthood of Jesus and an attentive listening to the experience of the poor will teach the Church how its mounting powerlessness might be life-changing and empowering.

Mission to or mission for?

> Yes, I'll give you that. Jesus is all right, but I'm not having anything to do with Church. They're not my sort of people. They're all middle class for a start. They can't help that but I can't get out of my house some days with all those cars parked round the church. They obviously come some distance – they're not from round here. They don't even look like us. Church doesn't work for people round here; we've got problems of our own thanks.

Ken was happy to help at the youth club but was very wary of any talk about church, especially if it seemed to be encroaching on the life of his estate. The poor have often experienced the mission of the Church as a quest for its own enlargement rather than an honouring of the community in which it is set and a seeking after God there. Bishop Adrian Newman fears that our nation's present obsession with economic growth has infected our understanding of what mission should be all about (Newman 2010). But we may very well ask, if Christian mission is primarily about the growth and strengthening of the Body of Christ, why did Jesus choose to take that body, bless it, break it, share it at the Last Supper and then give it away on the cross? The poor challenge the Church to give itself away in powerlessness for Christ's sake rather than build up its muscle for its own growth. In the Acts of the Apostles Luke, the writer, makes it clear that growth does come thick and fast, but only as a consequence of the Church giving itself away. We do not build the Church, but Christ will bless it in the way he pleases if we follow in his footsteps and give ourselves away. Numerical growth is a consequence of Kingdom mission, not its aim. The Dutch theologian and pastor Conrad Boerma has observed:

> There is historical evidence to show that the attraction of the first community did not lie in its missionary campaigns (there is virtually no call to evangelize in any of the epistles), but rather in its way of life . . . Without pretentious verbal claims, and simply by the way in which it broke down the barriers of class, race and sex, the church became a healing power in society . . . If people could live like this, their God must be very special (Boerma 1979, p. 94).

Ken tells me that what he sees of the local church he does not find attractive at all. But if he saw the local congregation giving itself away for the estate, what then might be his response? Derek Purnell, a member of Urban Presence, a very small unit of local estate Christians in Manchester, likes to quote Jesus' parable about a tiny portion of yeast hidden in a vast amount of flour leavening the whole batch (Matt. 13.33), and shares from his experience how a small but energized church congregation that is deeply embedded in a poor estate can be very influential across the whole community (Purnell 2003, p. 70). The only reason why Jesus told this yeast parable must surely have been because he envisioned small missional communities, not big ones for whom the parable would have been largely irrelevant. The poor teach us that when we are small and marginal, we are saved from presuming status and prestige in society, because we are simply in no position to be imperialistic in mission. In her extended essay *Three Guineas*, Virginia Woolf (1938) asserts that Christians only retain their unique quality if they remain 'free from servitude to their greatest temptation', which is to be 'insiders'. If Christians see themselves as part of the establishment and at one with the dominant values of our society, looking at the poor rather than being one with them, then they will have missed their prime vocation to be 'in pain yet always full of joy; poor and yet making many people rich; having nothing, and yet owning everything' (2 Cor. 6.10). This lesson is so hard to learn for a Church that over many centuries has been privileged with power and influence over vast reaches of the known world. To be forced back to the margins again and to live among the poor seems such a come-down, but may yet prove its salvation.

Placing ourselves in the company of the poor, and from that perspective looking carefully at Jesus' teaching makes us realize that they have a privileged place in his Kingdom – that way of living with God and one another that is made possible by the presence of Jesus Christ in the midst. We have only been able to touch upon a few examples of what the poor have to teach the Church when we adopt their hermeneutic of justice and utilize their contextual methodology, but perhaps even this small sample will have made us aware of what a revolution will be required of us all if the Church should follow its Lord's example and become poor so that others may be rich. Our task now must therefore be to consider just what that revolution might entail.

8

Incarnational Church?

What then are the changes that the Church itself, by God's grace, will have to make if it is to respond to this challenge? Clearly, we will not be able to get away with a slight adjustment here and a recalculation there, but profound realignment and substantial change of ethos will be required if the Church is to be reshaped according to the Kingdom values we have learned from the poor. But let us be clear, change of this magnitude cannot be left to the leaders of the Church, nor to the weakest of its members. For just as ministry is the shared responsibility of every baptized Christian, so also this revolutionary reformation of our Church is the task and responsibility of us all, acting together, so that no one should be lost. The Church, as the Body of Christ, is where all penitents rich and poor meet together in communion, recognizing one another as brothers and sisters in Christ. For note, in Luke's account no sooner has Jesus in his great sermon issued his proclamation of blessing upon the poor (Luke 6.20–23) and his warning Woes to the rich (vv. 24–26), than he turns to teaching us all that we must love one another absolutely and completely. There must be, says Jesus, no 'us and them' in the Kingdom, for we are truly all in this together. And he does not leave it there. We note that in verse 28 Jesus actually says: 'bless those that curse you'. Admittedly the word there is *eulogeite*, not the *Makarios* of the first Beatitude, but the challenge is clear. If you, the poor in your wretchedness, have been loved by God so much as to be pronounced blessed, then in the same way you must turn to the rich who have cursed you, bless them, and work with them to your mutual salvation and to the glory of God.

Then on completion of his sermon Jesus puts his words into action by going immediately to meet a foreigner, a rich and powerful centurion, to continue his work of healing a sick and divided world. All this lays a mandate upon us to hold true to one another as brothers and sisters in Christ, to reach across these barriers of ethnicity, otherness and even wealth, and work together for the profound change that we and our society require if we are to glimpse within it more signs of God's alternative Kingdom. Contextual theologians will also want to add that this determination to follow through from our theological reflection into concerted action is integral to the endeavour we call 'doing theology'. Just as prayer is only a mask if it does not lead to change, so theology that is not followed through in Kingdom action is sterile and certainly not contextual nor incarnational. Jesus offers his sermon, teaches a theology of the Kingdom and then is immediately back into acting it out at every step and with his every breath. So let us now take a deep breath, open our eyes wide and ask: what then must we do?

The Church forgets its Kingdom values

In order to determine how the Church should now respond, it's instructive to take a step back and look at the Church's story thus far. The early Christian converts were, as far as we can discern, from the poorer sections of society. Paul attests as he opens his letter to the Corinthians, 'not many of you are wise by human standards, not many influential, not many from noble families. No, God chose those who by human standards . . . are common and contemptible – indeed, those who count for nothing' (1 Cor. 1.26–28). But we can see from this that among the converts there were even then a tiny few who were not poor, and we have already noted that Jesus had among his own disciples some wealthy women who were prepared to fund the discipleship group (Luke 8.3). They had taken that radical step of sharing life with the poor and were even there at the crucifixion moment, already playing the part of servant, no doubt keeping the birds and dogs away from his dying body (Crossan 1995, p. 127). The famous passage in Acts 4.34–35 tells us that in the earliest days of the Church 'all those who owned land or houses would sell them, and bring the money from the sale of them, to present it to the apostles; it was then distributed to any who might be in need'. It seems to have been an economically inclusive society centred upon the situation of the poor, but that allowed the rich to play their part by getting down to earth with them and honouring the poor with whom they then shared. Paul's letters indicate, however, that this inclusivity was not always characteristic of all their gatherings, and he often has to remind them of the Kingdom values, because new converts had not yet come to terms with these new counter-cultural demands. Paul had noticed, for example, that even in their worship gatherings there was a tendency to grab at the shared food rather than respect the culture of equal sharing that their conversion now required (1 Cor. 11.17–22). But even Paul, great saint that he was, could not entirely escape the cultural pressures of his day. In his first letter to the Corinthian church for example, when he sets out his list of those who had witnessed the resurrection of Jesus, he names only the men, whereas our Gospel tradition is clear that it was Mary Magdalene who was the first witness, and it was she who told the men about the resurrection (1 Cor. 15.5–6, cf. John 20.18). It had obviously taken no time at all for even the leaders of the Church to begin to forget Christ's inclusive Kingdom values.

As time went on, this slippage continued, so that by the year 313 Constantine believed that when a Christian sign appeared to him in a vision the words that should accompany it were 'in this sign conquer!' He went on to do exactly that, killing and maiming to become the most powerful man in the Western world. And within 80 years, his empire had even become a violent persecutor of non-Christians. It fell to theologians like Augustine of Hippo to create a theology for this new dispensation, moving the Church from a movement at the margins of society to a dominating institution at its centre, presided over by a clerical caste. There was a move away from joyfulness to a concentration on our fallen nature and on judgement at the hands of a monarchical God.

Rather than the listening and inclusive style of Jesus, the Church now governed its people sternly, excluding those who did not toe the theological party line and punishing non-believers on the basis, as Augustine put it, that 'error has no rights'. Stuart Murray (now Stuart Murray Williams) tells us the sad story of this transformation from a Kingdom of God movement to the imperialism of institutionalized Christendom in his invaluable book *Post-Christendom* (Murray 2004). In it he spells out how that Christendom model has been perpetuated through the generations and even now leaves its heavy mark upon many aspects of the Church. We see it in the way it organizes and understands itself, the way it pictures God, and how it bases many of its decisions upon very worldly criteria rather than those of the alternative Kingdom. Put simply, Murray Williams sees Christendom as 'Christianity without Jesus at its centre'.

It is this Christendom form of Church that is the antithesis of all that the poor teach us about the Kingdom and that people in the West have recently begun to find so repugnant. They see the Church as being an institution they can well do without, an institution that seems to stand as a bastion against many of the human rights and values that modern democracies hold dear. Bishops are made Lords and wheeled out for state occasions, while their mission officers seem to speak more in terms of gaining market share than the revolutionary transformation of society Jesus espoused. Meanwhile, some non-denominational congregations blithely encroach imperialistically upon an area, introducing their own particular style of worship and authoritarian leadership, never thinking to listen and learn – Christendom is a mindset that is not just the prerogative of the established churches. Non-Christians have now become so accustomed to the élitism of the Churches that the media are astonished that the Pope has stooped so low as to make his own phone calls or that the Archbishop of Canterbury actually writes his own tweets.

In an age when institutions are neither trusted nor esteemed, the established denominations are very easy to criticize – and perhaps rightly so. But cumbersome institutions are only one manifestation of the more fundamental problem to which Murray Williams is alerting us. For although no Christian today would shed blood in the way Constantine was happy to do, the motto that could so easily be associated with many Christian groups and churches even now would still be that of Constantine's Christendom – 'in this sign conquer!' And why not? We know we have the truth – that we are right – so that gives our crusade legitimacy when we march into the lives and cultures of others, without any need to listen and learn, nor to concern ourselves that God may already be there in the hearts of those people. When European crusaders invaded the Holy Land we now know that they massacred untold numbers of Christians, on the assumption that all Arabs were infidels – they did not listen or learn. A Christendom culture's main concern is itself, even though it thinks that its concern is Jesus. The real problem with many an institution is therefore that its own culture has become more important to it than the service that it is there to render – and it is this 'power over' as opposed to 'power for' that has left so many churches unable to comprehend Jesus' teaching that it is actually the poor, the weak, the outsider, who must be in the vanguard of all its endeavours.

While many church people are constrained to soak up their energies with concerns for the maintenance and furtherance of their organizations, those outside the faith look on with varying degrees of exasperation, outrage or indifference. Many non-church people happen to have heard about Jesus and are seriously impressed by him and think he may have things of consequence to share, but they would rather look him up on Google than trust the Church to teach them more. Those who are on the inside of the Church try so very hard to bridge the gap but are made to think that by continuing to do the same old things but with more vigour, or with a more contemporary style, all will come right. But the world is challenging the Church to remember the poor man who rode a donkey into Jerusalem. And many a local congregation do indeed accomplish wonderful things, and the commitment of individual Christians can often be very inspiring – and just a few do bridge that gap between the Church and those that look on, by outstanding acts of selflessness – but too many are being held back or even misdirected by a mindset that has forgotten the power of the Beatitudes.

Living in the *kairos* moment

I believe the Church is confronted by two choices. We can bury our heads in the sand and keep working to this Christendom model which is exhausting us all with its resultant medieval institutions and is such a turn-off for most Western people, or we can see this growing mistrust of the Christendom model as a *kairos* moment – a God-given opportunity to think again about what sort of Church God wants. The first option is preferred by many Christians since it requires very little risk or immediate change. The top-down approach still promises a degree of prestige and status and might just stand up for one more generation before it topples over for ever. I call this 'the one-generation option'. But the post-Christendom generation, which is fast forming, no longer believes that the Church has a right to be at the centre or to be listened to with respect. It seems to them to be populated by anoraks who deny the findings of science, are obsessed with sexuality, sing songs that have a rather Disneyland quality about them, believe themselves to be better than others, and are good to have on great occasions because some of their leaders dress like wizards. They speak about God but in words that cannot be understood. If the reader should think me rather cynical here, let me be clear that I love the Church and am very happy to dress like a wizard too on occasion, but these criticisms are drawn from real surveys – it's clear that the Church simply mystifies the post-Christendom generation. Whenever our church-centred mindset hampers our primary vocation in this way, making us seem more concerned for ourselves than for the Kingdom, then we must hear the alarm bells ringing and take that second option – to muster for decisive reform.

We are now in a post-Christendom era, even if the Church at large has not yet been able to own it, but on the poor housing estates this reality is as clear as day. At the very beginning of this book I explained why I had chosen to look especially at housing estates rather than elsewhere in order to understand the poor, but let me now add the final reason why the poor housing estates are today so crucial to the Kingdom. It is that it is here that we will find Christians who have already been battling with this post-Christendom challenge for a very long time. They have deep and long-term experience of working with many generations who are not simply un-Churched, nor even anti-Church, but for whom Church is nowhere on their radar and never has been. On one of my visits I was told:

> If I started to talk about the Christian faith to these people, they would have no hooks to hang it on. This is why a lot of estate church congregations are not from the estate but are people who have moved out and come back only on Sundays. Even they don't understand what it's like here now. Today you start from nothing. But that makes it very exciting, because quite frankly they don't have to unlearn all the Sunday School rubbish the Church used to teach. You can introduce them fresh to the real Jesus. The problem is that they then get excited about Jesus, they go along to the local church, and it doesn't connect with what they've just experienced of him. The local church seems to be living in another era.

The urban poor have always been in the vanguard of post-Christendom, since they had little or nothing to gain from the imperialistic ways of the old mindset or of its institutions. But now the tables have turned and Christians of all sorts have everything to gain from the poor housing estate churches, seizing the *kairos* moment and learning from them how to create the servant Church for a new era.

Deep listening

In *Urban Ministry and the Kingdom of God* (Green 2003), I devote a chapter to the history of urban mission in Britain and name many of the courageous and wonderful people who have worked so hard through the years to bring the concerns of the poor to the centre of the Church's life. But over time the institution and the Christendom mindset have very often quietened their initiatives and softened their impact. It makes us realize that until we shift the Church at large from its old ways even our great movements will only result in tinkering at the edges. We seem to try repeatedly to put new wine into old crumbling wineskins.

Our first step must therefore be, as we have been realizing, to encourage more Christians to place themselves alongside the poor, not this time so much to serve them as to listen and to learn from them. This will put us on the road to renegotiating our identity as Church. We may have to go through a process similar to that of the older son in the story of the Prodigal (Luke 15.25–32). He considers himself to have been the bastion of faithfulness through the years, but on the return of the Prodigal, he has to come to terms with the fact that the whole household is not just accommodating his returning brother, but his new presence is restructuring the family so that each member's identity has to be renegotiated. And as we engage in this renegotiation we will probably find our past being judged by critical voices from the Bible. For example, the more we look honestly at our present allegiance to the Christendom model of Church the more we will come to recognize ourselves in the Pharisees of the Gospels – those sticklers for orthodoxy and adherence to the regulations. They demanded that everyone should keep the Ten Commandments, especially observance of the Sabbath, but Jesus knew from living with the poor that not working on the Sabbath meant the loss of a vital day's wage for them. But the Pharisees were probably quite unaware of how their religious obsessions had blinded them to their own oppression of the poor. Jesus therefore taught them that the Sabbath was there to serve the people, not people the Sabbath (Mark 2.27). And he is teaching us today that the Church is similarly there to serve the people, not that people should serve the Church. Why then do we ask our laypeople to show how Christian they are, not by moving out to love their neighbours but by engaging in church activities and helping the vicar maintain the organization? The time has surely come to attend to the non-Christendom voice of Jesus and listen to the poor with a repentant attitude.

Reasons for confidence

If we can muster the courage to acknowledge the Church's predicament and own the fact that we are part of the problem, this properly repentant attitude will free us to enjoy glimpses of the Kingdom breaking into the situation. To begin with, parts of the Church have already made this cultural transition and are only too willing to share their treasures with us. Many of the poorest estates are inhabited by committed Christian laypeople and superb ordained staff, all with deep and significant experience. They are used to utilizing empowerment styles of leadership, have been deeply embedded within the community through thick and thin, and know where to find the most sustaining spiritual resources. They will teach us how to wait upon God, will already have developed many alternative methods of organizing themselves, and will have devised more apt liturgies.[1] They will be adept at sorting the wheat from the chaff when it comes to resources, and will know how to create their own. They will also be masters of sustaining ministry on a shoestring. They may have let their skills of verbal articulation atrophy in a culture where that is not prized, but they will have wisdom well worth attending to.

We can have confidence too, because even at the higher levels of the Church, there is a growing awareness of the problem – if only brought on by concern about the catastrophic fall in church attendance.[2] There is also a burgeoning commitment to indigenous lay leadership, although it will still be necessary to redesign the very middle-class models of training at present on offer. There is certainly an appreciation of the need to appoint supportive team ministries, a new ecumenical openness to learning from all quarters, and a clear recognition that we can gain from the vast array of different spiritual and liturgical traditions that are there to sustain us. We can have confidence too in the sacraments of the

1 The concept of 'apt liturgy' was developed by Ann Morisy, especially in *Journeying Out* (2004), Chapter 8.

2 For example, the Church of England is currently embarking on a programme of reform and renewal entitled *In Each Generation*, which at this early stage seems to be a helpful first step.

Church, which speak directly and unequivocally of the Kingdom's sharing culture, gathering us as one body to share broken bread, or have our common identity in Christ affirmed through our one baptism. It would appear that just when God is challenging the Church with a *kairos* moment, God is also providing us with the resources to listen, risk and respond. Now we must have the confidence to be guided by the poor to use those God-given resources well.

But the Christendom model is still alive and well when churches make decisions such as the closure of an estate church on the basis not of Kingdom values, but merely because it does not measure up to bureaucratic financial or numeric criteria or fit in with the latest diocesan plan for efficiency. But in Birmingham, Bradford, Newcastle, Manchester, Sheffield and elsewhere, ministers and laity from poor estates are meeting regularly to do theology together, so that they may be better equipped to place Jesus always at the centre of their decision-making. It is theology steeped in prayer and sternly underpinned by study and embedded experience. In Birmingham, for example, one of these groups has published a booklet called *Strengthening Estate Ministry – Thriving in Mission* (Barrett and Delmege 2011), in which they demonstrate how God's mission can be discerned time and again in their estates, and how being at the margins of society can help them better appreciate the teaching and work of Jesus. They are constructing a fascinating Kingdom theology from which to make their decisions for the wellbeing of their communities and their church. Another group has been studying the account of the appearance of the risen Jesus recorded in John's Gospel (John 20.19–25), noting that when the Disciples shut themselves away from the locals for fear of violence, Jesus was in their midst, showing them the scars of his crucifixion, as if to say, 'Here are my credentials – I really am with you in this, and we can make it through together.' This has given them new courage and a determination to move forward on their estates. Despite the challenges of a post-Christendom culture, signs of confidence and glimpses of the Kingdom are springing up everywhere.

The elephant in the room

The aristocratic British journalist Peregrine Worsthorne went to the nub of it when he once said: 'There is no such thing as a class war, and we are determined to win it!' It has been extensively argued that there is now no such thing as class, even though according to the 2013 British Social Attitudes Survey six out of ten people designate themselves as working class. Marx defined class in terms of our relationship to the means of production, modern economists compare income and wealth ratios, cultural commentators look to lifestyle, geographers to social space; but while definitions vary, if you are poor, you know that on all these counts your life is very different from those at the other end of the spectrum, and in nearly every aspect of your life those at the other end will be making decisions about your life, and you will have no say about theirs. And while Jesus places himself at the poor end of this spectrum, the Church is largely representative of those at the other end. Even those denominations that were once proud of being very working class have found themselves 'moving up and moving out'. So when the clergy of the poor estates complain to their denominations that the liturgies and resources provided to them by the national Church simply do not work for their congregations, the national Church still seems able only to offer them what suits middle-class tastes. Similarly, poor congregations are expected by their sponsoring churches to elect individuals to positions of leadership to run meetings on very middle-class lines with churchy agendas, and to take on paperwork that really does not suit them. And when these inappropriate strait-jackets prove unsuccessful, the poor churches are judged to be deficient or even not viable, and the pressures are on for closure. Poor congregations battle on as best they can trying to fulfil the institution's requirements, but knowing things are stacked against them. I met this scenario so often on my travels that I found it quite depressing to see local gifts and talents being debilitated by the steady drip of unnecessary and ill-fitting expectations from above.

But we must not become defeatist about this gap in understanding and communication between classes, because in today's globalizing world we are learning that cultures are no longer as impermeable as they once were. Across the globe many people today know themselves to be hybrid, and some find it difficult, just as Mercy did in our second chapter, to pigeon-hole themselves into just one culture or class. Cultures are not the silos that we once took them to be, and I count myself among many who move easily between the British working- and middle-class cultures, so that collectively they are well-placed to act as champions and interpreters of the oppressed in both camps. On the road to justice, both have gifts to offer in an egalitarian Church.

Travelling light

I've noticed that as my friends get older, they are apt to say that they believe more and more in less and less, for gone is the anguish over concerns we once held to be so important, for we now perceive them to have been more to do with our own immature need to be right than with the values of the Kingdom. A faith liberated from a Christendom mindset will save us having to wait till we are all old, before we come to the same realization that so little of the church-centred agenda really matters. This liberation will leave the Church freer and more agile for mission and allow Christian congregations to direct their energies towards discerning the presence of God in their local communities and in their worship.

Knowing what church regulations to retain and what to jettison will demand a negotiation between the hermeneutic of order and the hermeneutic of justice, for if order controls at the expense of justice we are back with the Christendom model hampering our every move, but just the right degree of order will keep us together as a Christian family, safeguard our catholicity, and keep us accountable to ethical standards. Meanwhile, a less controlling system would allow the local congregation to decide how best to manage its affairs and to work a more collegial form of shared leadership.

One thing that Jesus talks about a great deal is money. He talks of giving it away, sharing it, and never letting it dominate our decisions or our lives, for we 'cannot be the slave both of God and of money' (Matt. 6.24). The Church of England has a deep commitment to sharing across all its parishes, each contributing to the common pot according to its ability and receiving according to its need. But just as in the New Testament Church, there are still squabbles about how just the calculations are that determine each contribution. But we must be clear that given the present economic structures of society, poor congregations will never be in a position to be financially self-sufficient. They will always have to rely on grants and subsidies. So the injection of funds for a short term on condition that a poor church becomes larger and financially self-sufficient is to judge on inappropriate criteria, even though it is increasingly the condition upon which cash injections are granted. If a poor church does manage to grow its congregation substantially, it will then be full of even more people who have no cash to offer but more needs to be attended to. If a wealthy church increases in size, it should be able to afford to give even more money away and do with fewer clergy. The two cases are entirely different, but Christendom churches are apt to use the same criteria to judge both situations, so that the poor church's financial balance sheet always appears to show the congregation is failing, when maybe they are excelling in Kingdom commitment. What getting alongside the poor will teach the Church at large is how beneficial it will be to invest financially in supporting their work nevertheless, because they will repay the wider Church – not financially, to be sure, but in delivering for it a spiritual harvest a thousand-fold.

Many young Christians today are learning this lesson and putting the old Church to shame by offering substantial years of their lives to serving on a self-funding basis in very poor areas. While the Christendom Church still has a revolution ahead of it, it is more than encouraging to see this new generation's commitment to the Jesus of the poor. They are not burdened by that old mindset, and they are learning that being with the poor and learning from them will help create a Church fit for purpose.

Incarnational mission

It used to be that churches would talk about mission as 'outreach' – reaching out to others from where we are. Incarnational mission works the other way round. It begins where others are and, as with Jesus on the road to Emmaus, we hope to be invited in. The whole of Acts 10 is devoted to a description of the invitation Peter receives from a Gentile centurion called Cornelius. Although it means stepping into an alien culture, Peter readily goes to his house, because he has received a vision revealing God's intention that the emerging Church must be a totally inclusive one. So he risks involvement with Cornelius and his household, and when asked to address them, he begins by saying: 'I now really understand' (v. 34). Peter, the great missionary, has realized that his evangelistic visit was primarily intended by God to convert him! He returns to share his experience with the Jerusalem church, and that proves to be a conversion of the whole Church, as is demonstrated by the rest of the Acts of the Apostles. The Church must know that God is already active in the world, often in alien places, and our missional task is not so much to get people into church as to get the Church out, alongside God in the world, to join in God's mission there.

But even this has to be done with great sensitivity. John Hayes now lives on a Bangladeshi estate in Shadwell Gardens, East London, but one of his enormous artworks is an exquisitely drawn canvas of a slum settlement in Cambodia, where he previously ministered for some years. Hovering over the slum he has drawn an intimidating helicopter gun-ship dominating the skies. From its undercarriage is slung not the expected cluster-bomb, but an enormous effigy of Jesus holding out his arms in blessing. It is a figurative representation of what John sees as the worst kind of evangelism – the dominating imposition of our own religious culture upon the vulnerable. The drawing begs us to think twice before we parachute ourselves into the cultures of the poor and tell them, on our terms, how good our own take on the gospel is. John's Mission Order, innerCHANGE, describes its own approach to mission in this way:

> The Upside-Down Kingdom: We will minister low to high, that is, from the bottom rungs of a society upward, remembering that significant aspects of God's kingdom are often lodged in the humblest crevices. We will not despise faithfulness to small things in favour of the big picture, believing that the kingdom of God is upside down with regard to many of the world's values.[3]

The incarnation of Jesus shows that even God refuses to act in a top-down fashion but chooses instead to be born to a vulnerable family so as to redeem the world from within. And God only did that when the people themselves were crying out for this visit; Jesus stands at the door and knocks, but never barges in – Kingdom values forbid the self-indulgent Christendom model of mission. The old traditional picture of the parish priest living in the midst of the community for many years, experiencing life alongside the people, immersed in a worshipping community committed to acting in faith, is a picture of what was often a gracious ministry – subverting from within the dominant Christendom model that could so easily have overwhelmed it.

Jane Winter has long been committed to housing estate ministry but tells of one experience where it was decided from above that a new broom would offer the housing estate congregation a new lease of life. A consultation took place in which the locals were offered all they could hope for, but at the price of no longer leading the mission themselves. What they got was a Bishop's Mission Order authorizing leadership from a thriving suburban church nearby. But, Jane reports, the newcomers 'have imported an expression of worship which lacks cultural sensitivity. The class distinction has become more acute. They speak of empowerment and participation but model take-over on their terms. It all reflects an age old tension for the Church of being contextually relevant while bound to a tradition and hierarchical structure drawn from the middle and upper classes' (Winter 2014). Those who embark on this 'journey downwards' to be alongside the poor must realize that the conversion God is looking for is their own! Those who do

3 www.innerchange.org.

this well have realized that a 'mission-shaped church' is not one that merely experiments with alternative forms of worship and aggressive planning, but is a radically changed institution that is incarnated with the poor and takes its lead from its embeddedness with them.

Working together

Eleven years of my life were spent very happily within a congregation of Methodists, Anglicans and others on an estate in the back streets of Birmingham. When asked why the ecumenical partnership was going so well, I would explain that it was because we rarely spent time looking at our doctrinal or liturgical differences, we just took them as given and directed all our attention and energies to getting out into the community. Pope Francis and Archbishop Justin seem to be getting on so well for the very same reason. There are so many pressing issues in God's world that spending time on institutional rivalry is belittling of those who really need our attention.

Judith Wray is a very experienced Methodist deacon, who was asked to undertake ministry on a tough estate but once there realized she had not been given the support she had been promised. She wrote later: 'Thank God for Sheila from the United Reformed church and for Susan from the Anglican church – both of whom lived on the estate and were so keen to grasp the nettle.' The other denominations themselves were very suspicious, because Judith's post had been advertised as a church plant, not giving credit to the fact that their own churches had been ministering there for years. But after a fretful start the denominations learned not to get in a tizz, and they now work well together. We need each other so much, but will only be able to operate together if we jettison the remnants of that old defensiveness and our imperialist denominational mindset. Both debilitate the mission, disgrace ourselves and ignore the poor.

A remarkable resurgence of life is taking place across the Church within the evangelical community which is sensing a strong vocation to our poor housing estates. Some 20 years ago, when this first began to surface, the movement was naïve, romantic and self-centred, and many who came across their experiments were appalled. They heard these incomers speaking in terms of 'taking Jesus to the poor', converting the vulnerable, and pulling up the local culture by its bootstraps. But a very significant change has occurred through these years and now warrants our best attention.[4] There remain many examples of bad practice, but others have learned their lessons through experience and now have much to teach the wider Church about incarnational mission, long-term commitment, appropriate preparation and training, and non-intrusive ways of sharing one's faith. Urban Expression are doing great things, while Churches Together are sponsoring food-banks and street pastorates, and the Eden Network is working among the young. Reaching the Unreached has adopted radical working-class culture and the broad coalitions of Hope Together and Gather are offering fresh expressions of ecumenism. The excitement is infecting many parts of the Church with the Anglican-inspired Church Urban Fund still proving extraordinarily creative, and the Roman Catholic and Anglican religious orders putting nuns and friars into the front line of mission. Many of the new initiatives are working hand in glove with their parish churches and finding that differing spiritual and liturgical styles need not hinder the mission if all are working to Kingdom values.

Many of the best and most appropriate resources for estate churches are currently being produced by such groups as these, working across denominational boundaries. But there remains mistrust and scepticism, prompting Stuart Murray Williams to write from the perspective of the new churches: 'Emerging churches need the theological and historical insights, accumulated wisdom and traditions of inherited churches. Inherited churches need the stimulus, provocation, pioneering and creative cultural engagement

---

4 See, for example, Anna Thompson's excellent research paper 'Holy Sofas' (2012), which highlights the Eden Network's learning and increasing maturity based on its substantial experience of relocating young volunteers into urban communities.

of emerging churches' (Murray 2004, pp. 255–6). If we can learn to relate as critical friends, open to one another's insights and honestly sharing our own, the poor would benefit, and we could all mature together.

Engaging politically

A large proportion of the Hebrew Scriptures concerns the relationship between faith and politics. It is good then to see that one of the greatest strengths of the denominational churches is that they are prepared to engage the political world, even at the highest national and international levels, and do so with some vigour in order to address the causes of injustice rather than attend only to local symptoms. In the tradition of the prophets, they endeavour to speak the truth to power and are sometimes not thanked for doing so. This is all part of the healing ministry of the Church – seeking to bring wholeness, reconciliation, justice and maturity to fraught situations. At Braunstone in Leicester, it took the intervention of the vicar and the archdeacon to sort out an almighty row between the local authority and the estate community over the workings of a New Deal initiative. As I write, many Anglican bishops are prompted by what they see and learn from visiting their parishes and projects to speak out nationally about the issues they raise and, in response to predatory loan sharks, the Church of England is rolling out a programme of credit union facilities across the country and is keenly engaged with others, not least the Roman Catholic Diocese of Westminster, in seeking to reintroduce a strong ethical compass for modern business corporations and finance houses (Sentamu 2015). That the denominations are engaged in such creative critique is a very welcome measure of how seriously they take their prophetic role, and to do so in a servant-like post-Christendom manner takes tremendous courage and an aversion to the seductive lure of power. The dangers are all too real, for as the Lord's Prayer has taught us, evil can so easily infect our political and institutional structures and compromise those who come close to them. Again, we will find that the very best way to guard against these dangers is to make our home with the poor, who will not allow us to forget on whose behalf the prophet acts.

Other Christian projects also seek to engage politically. The Church Urban Fund remains one of those treasures of the Church that spans the gulf between the poor and the powerful in many ways, not least through the very well-informed briefing papers it publishes and its supportive programmes across the country. Our own NECN, the National Estate Churches Network, seeks to voice the concerns of the poor estates to the powers that be, and some of their national conferences have included debates with national and local politicians and developers, giving the poor opportunity to put their concerns forward on welfare, housing and development policy.

Increasingly, political and community engagement is taking place at a much more local level too because of the new preparedness of local social care and local government agencies to partner with local Christian communities. This is to some extent due to the fact that they themselves have been so debilitated by cut-backs that they are less able to maintain a go-it-alone attitude. But if local congregations are to respond to these overtures, they need administrative assistance and specialist training in order that all may benefit from these partnerships without the church compromising its distinctive purpose and presence. It is so easy to be manipulated by other agencies into becoming their service providers. There are many traps along the way for the unwary, but mission of any sort has always been fraught with risks and dangers alongside its many rewards. All should be well, if the post-Christendom Church holds true to its Kingdom values and takes its steer from the Jesus of the poor.

Redirecting resources

When the Church gives itself away, it stays true to its founder, and he grows the Church. It is therefore not a waste, but instead an investment, to redirect our resources towards the poor. It fulfils our Lord's teaching and, as we have seen, continues the practice of the New Testament Church. We spoke earlier of sharing our money, but the Church's greatest resource is actually its people, whose unflagging commitment warrants resourcing and training of the highest calibre. The model of learning that the poor usually favour is that of group apprenticeship – a few friends working together with a mentor for on-the-job training and group reflection. Investment in this style, with a written-in expectation that power would be given into the hands of those thus successfully trained, would be a great encouragement to poor churches. But too much of the training on offer is designed to teach laypeople how to take over churchy tasks rather than to be the Church's front-line troops out in their communities. Often, the Church has built itself an overly bureaucratic structure that demands that the talents and energies of each congregation are used up in keeping the machine running. Often, however, the estate congregation will boast skills of an altogether different nature, and finding themselves unable to cope thus feel oppressed by these bureaucratic demands. This encourages those who moved out from the estate years ago to return to 'help' their former parish, but then they take over, only serving to devalue further the local skills and stifle local lay development.

It's good for each congregation to work out the best style of operation for its own context, but my suggestion might be that each should be equipped by the wider Church with an administrator to take on such book-keeping, secretarial and form-filling responsibilities as are absolutely necessary, releasing the laity and clergy to be the front-line troops out in the community. Each congregation would also need to be introduced to the treasures and traditions of the Church, especially Bible and Sacrament, and to gain experience in the contextual theological method. If this is done by an ordained minister, they must be appropriately trained and skilled for work in this specific context and with those particular people. The denominations need to direct significant investment in creating support resources for the development of the laity and clergy together, not based upon middle-class assumptions but utilizing the particular expertise of those on the poor estates – recognizing those gifts and skills we have touched upon in the body of this study. The

Church should make sure that ministry groups in areas of poverty are very well resourced, since they have suffered from a history of under-investment through so many years.

Michael Hirst, a retired researcher writing in the *Methodist Recorder* in 2012 (Hirst 2012, p. 8), calculated that for his own denomination: 'At least 18 per cent of ministers would have to move to a more deprived area if they were to be evenly distributed across the five levels of deprivation' – a scale grading areas from the most deprived to the most affluent. What's more, he calculated that over half of the ministers were living in the two most affluent bands in the country. These figures make it clear that the denominations are investing their clerical resources in those areas that probably least need that expertise. This certainly helps to maintain those wealthy areas where the Christendom style flourishes, but it will be at the expense of all that our study of the Beatitudes has taught us. Michael Hirst called his article 'Location, Location, Location', commenting: 'Where we live reflects how we see ourselves and shapes how others see us. Theological reflection may also be influenced by, and expressed through, where we live.' If he's right, then it will not only be how they are currently trained, but also where they are housed that will distance our clergy from where the Kingdom Church needs them to be.

Staying for a moment with the issue of training, many of the clergy who now work in poor housing estates feel that the atmosphere surrounding the training they received in colleges and courses was so class-specific that the theology imbibed, the spirituality inculcated and the skills being taught were overlaid with an inappropriate style, so that when they found themselves alongside the poor they had to 'unlearn' these things in order to engage properly with their new context. Some course teachers themselves feel uncomfortable about their work and have been telling me that it is not so much that people from poor communities struggle with the theology, but that they find the methods of assessment, teaching and learning so alien. When they move back into ministry, they find they have been deskilled and, by default, begin to promote the course's Christendom models, quite against their better nature. It is frightening too that rarely can those preparing for ordination in the inherited churches have opportunity to live on deprived estates during training and learn their theology there. And as I have said before, it is always dangerous to formulate theology at a distance from the poor.

Finally, there is the resource of church buildings. I'm told that around the country our buildings are in better repair today than they have ever been in British history, but you would never believe that to look at most housing estate church premises. They often look uninviting from the outside, and inside they are tatty and lack investment. Yet these churches and halls are very often the only gathering places remaining on the estates, where even the pubs are fast closing. Local building skills plus injections of money from sponsors and denominations could work wonders, and this would give the poor encouraging affirmation and the wherewithal to move forward into all sorts of exciting mission.

Mary's revolutionary challenge

We have rehearsed just a few of the ways in which our Christian Church needs to untangle itself from its murky Christendom past and embrace a new Kingdom future based upon all that we learn together from the poor. There are many glimpses of the new possibilities to be had, and the Holy Spirit has been very forgiving in letting even our half-hearted attempts bear fruit. Our difficulty, though, is in the scale of the challenge for, as has become clear, to allow the poor their rightful place as the vanguard of the Kingdom will require not just tinkering but profound cultural change at the heart of all our churches. This is exemplified once again in Mary's Kingdom song, the Magnificat.

Luke (Luke 1.46–55, NRSV) has her begin her song with the words: 'My soul magnifies the Lord', indicating her personal reorientation away from the old self and towards her Lord. Each of us will likewise be required to turn from the inward-looking culture of Christendom and towards the Kingdom values of our Lord Jesus. And as well as praying for this personal revolution, her song then takes us from that level to the social plane where a revolution is also anticipated – 'all generations will call me blessed'. She, with all the poor she represents, will now be acknowledged as at the forefront of the Kingdom's agenda. There will be a political revolution required of us too – 'He has brought down the powerful from their thrones' – a rethink on how we organize our society and our Church. Next her song points us to an economic revolution – 'he has filled the hungry with good things, and sent the rich away empty'. And it finally demands that our Kingdom revolution has an ecologically sustainable future – 'to his descendants for ever'.

Mary's song tells us that these five arenas of life will all have to be restructured if we are bold enough to acknowledge the implications of her Son's pronouncement that the poor are blessed and for us to learn from them. It will demand a revolutionary change for all of us in which the Christendom mindset will have no place.

9

The Vanguard of the Kingdom

In these chapters, we have travelled together all around the 'doing theology cycle', until now we arrive back with the people of the estate – those to whom we listened when we first began. We listened to their voices and looked at their history, and from that context we prayed through the Lord's Prayer, finding there the radical Jesus of the Poor pointing us towards the values of his Kingdom. But we have realized that the institutions of our Church have not always developed in accordance with those values and have adopted Christendom styles that have blinded us to the revolution Jesus called for. We have studied our Lord Jesus' teaching that the poor are especially blessed, and that has led us back to a better recognition of the life we should be leading and the direction our Church should be following. Charged with these insights, we now re-join our sisters and brothers in our estate churches to consider the local practicalities of a Kingdom response.

Claiming the inheritance

Dotty poured me a second cup of tea and set it down in front of me on the kitchen table. She sat down and stared out of the window, thinking carefully about my question. She looked up and said:

> Yes, I think he's right. The poor are blessed, although a lot of 'em don't want to know it. Not that being poor's much fun, believe me, but it does make me feel very close to God somehow. Funny, isn't it. I've got such friends, you see. We're all in

> the same boat. But I remember the vicar saying, Jesus is in the same boat with us. I don't think rich people would understand.

She giggled and said, 'I wouldn't mind having some of their money though, would you?'

Other poor estate tenants were not at all sure about being blessed, although most of those I asked who were Christians had an inkling that Jesus was right. But even they would voice their reluctance by saying: 'But we don't have much to offer, do we?' If the poor are going to claim their inheritance as the blessed of the Kingdom, the first piece of good news they need to hear is that they do indeed have much to offer. Poor people have amazing gifts but have been encouraged to think that they don't. Many have significant manual skills and a readiness to use them; they know how to make a little go a long way; they know their area better than others and they know its hidden networks. They know the realities of injustice; where to get things more cheaply and how to keep going when others would have thrown in the towel. What some poorer communities do find difficult are those tasks that many churches ask of them, such as accountancy and committee skills. Trades unions and working men's clubs were often very good at training people in these tasks, but those organizations are now rare. So perhaps it is helpful, at least initially, to reaffirm the poor's blessedness by working from the skills they do have within the community rather than continuing to bemoan the absence of skills they don't have. The people of the ecumenical parish church on the Hodge Hill Estate in Birmingham were fed up with hearing negative descriptions of their community and wanted instead to affirm the many positive things about Hodge Hill. They went to shops, pubs, schools and all manner of community hubs to gather nominations for their Hodge Hill Unsung Heroes campaign. They then visited all the 97 local 'heroes' who had been nominated and brought them together for a grand prize-giving supper. Out of this affirming event has grown a whole battery of community initiatives based on the gifts the estate clearly does have, and since then many things have flourished and added sparkle to the life of Hodge Hill

(Barrett 2013). By affirming the gifts and skills hidden within the community rather than only accentuating the needs and negative aspects of the area, they began to recognize the truth of which Jesus had assured them – that the poor are blessed.

One of the joys of being a parish priest is to witness the extraordinary ability of even the poorest congregation to create a sense of community solidarity. Steve came to the vicarage door in Leicester to thank Father Tony for the way he had conducted his son's untimely funeral. He wanted to repay the kindness by opening a breakfast club in the spacious church lobby. Two years later the place is buzzing each morning with community life and 'full English' breakfasts. The vulnerable are fed, lonely mums bring their toddlers, and hoodies help clear the tables. In other places, there are football teams, karate clubs, DVD groups, BMX and skateboard clubs, shared lunches, music groups, bring and buy parties – such things flourish in many poor communities and the necessary community leadership emerges from the most unexpected quarters. As at the breakfast club, the churches often have the asset of accommodation to share and somewhere on the network will be those who are happy to offer their skills to smarten up what might be a lacklustre church hall, if they know it is going to be put to good use.

It is one thing to be designated 'blessed', but something altogether different to claim that inheritance and make it one's own. So the strengthening of these community networks and groups is a foundational step on the way to building the self-confident awareness the poor have had drained from them. Some Christians continue to lock themselves away behind closed doors for fear, like the first disciples before they fully realized the power of the resurrection (John 20.19), but it is important that the local Christian congregation is thoroughly integrated into those community networks in every way possible, celebrating the blessedness. Christians need not fear getting out of church and becoming one with God at work in the local community groups. But as well as being very much part of this wider affirmation of community gifts, the Christian congregation will have its own special contribution to make too.

The small church

The Christian group or congregation may not be very large on the estate, but as we've said, like the yeast, if it is deeply embedded in the networks of the community, its influence can be out of all proportion to its size. And its task will in some ways be quite simple – to become intimately aware of God's presence all around the community, to worship God with all their heart, to seek out what God is wanting done in the community, joining in that work, and so giving thanks for glimpses of God's Kingdom come. In essence, we are there, as Jesus has commanded, to love God with all our heart and to love our neighbours as ourselves (Mark 12.30–31).

But of course this is always more challenging than it sounds and for a small congregation it may seem quite daunting, even though a small estate church may actually have some advantages over the large thriving one. First, their vulnerability is probably more representative of its locality than if it were strong and flourishing, and it will be less likely to be pretentious. It may additionally be more committed to a counter-cultural life, and as long as it is not overburdened with finance, bureaucracy and buildings, may be free to think outside the box. But perhaps where the small Christian group or congregation really scores is in the intimacy of its close, supportive relationships. Anyone living in a poor community needs a supportive group or family network if they are not to be beaten by the relentless challenges of their surroundings. Nita told me that her experience had taught her that 'ministry on this estate is like running a marathon, so a supportive small congregation or team to care and cover for one another is a godsend'. Of course, a small group can sometimes itself be quite draining and in need of a lot of nurturing, but work put in on strengthening relationships bears dividends in the long term, saving individuals from burning out or becoming depressed. But negativity can overwhelm any of us, and so it is the duty of parent denominations or networks to ensure that every estate church has top-quality support, just as Jesus supported his own discipleship group when tensions arose.

A small estate congregation can offer essential mutual support but can also harbour difficulties, not least if it becomes a safe haven for a small band who have become inward-looking and fearful of venturing out into the community. They can pull up the drawbridge and lock the doors. A little congregation can also become dominated by its most cantankerous members if the spiritual maturity of the community has been sapped over the years. Group work and community activity are usually the most creative antidotes to these problems for, when reaching out to others, power has to be shared and the recognition of others' gifts is strongly fostered. And when all goes well a small indigenous congregation can perform wonders, as is evident at Coverdale Baptist Church in Manchester, where there is no paid minister and only a really tiny, committed congregation, but the place is buzzing almost 24/7 in Christian witness to the estate.

Within even a small estate congregation there will be vast differences of outlook and temperament, and this can be a great asset as long as they are openly shared, so that they can be understood by all. Kate Pearson (2014) writes:

> I do not love the drug-taking and dealing in the alleyway next to our house, nor the regular vandalism of anything we try and do in the area. But I do love the reckless abandon with which the young people dance on the roof of our church hall; the informal games of football on our front lawn and meeting six people on the way to the shops . . . and I love our church . . . which perhaps like a grandmother's front room, is well past its best but is loved and cherished.

Wallace and Mary Brown, however, write from their experience, 'It is a terrible fact that godlessness reigns supreme over the council estates . . . and a lingering death of our churches. Where is the taste of a growing church?' (Brown and Brown undated, p. 19). Kate, Wallace and Mary are all fine ministers, but they have been predisposed to interpret their experiences differently. If the Christian community is to benefit from these seeming contradictions, it simply must make space for honest and respectful sharing. How is this to be done?

It's all about relationships

Even if we belong to a larger congregation, it will be important to meet regularly in small groups, for it is only within that intimacy that much of our deeper learning will take place. If participants are reluctant to visit other people's homes, a 'cosy corner' can be created in the church or hall, and a gentle welcoming atmosphere will allow for members to get to know one another, perhaps by sharing their favourite DVDs or TV soaps and discussing what part Jesus could play if he became one of the characters in the drama.[1] As things progress and confidence builds, it becomes possible to look at the Gospel stories and share at a more personal level about their implications for our lives. And while all this is happening in the group it will be very important to keep in close relationship with one another and fully engaged in the community networks, so that the connections can be made between our growing Christian faith and what is happening on the estate and in the life of the church. I've described many ways that this can be done in *Let's Do Theology* (Green 2009).

The small group will also display its specifically Christian character by worshipping together, and with the larger congregation if there is one. The worship need not be complex nor led by an ordained minister, but wherever it occurs it is imperative that access is easy, that participants are welcomed, and that the toilets are clean. A welcoming atmosphere is enhanced by music and a loud enough amplifier and speakers can usually be borrowed or bought in a charity shop, while many Christian CDs come with downloadable words either for singing along or for reflection. The set-up can be a simple 'round the kitchen table' grouping, café-style tables or a circle of chairs, or if numbers are greater,

1 A fine set of openers for a variety of small groups is published by www.table-talk.org.

slightly inclined rows of chairs will save the very shy from having to look into the faces of others. Each group will devise what works best for them, and we'll say more about estate worship in a moment, but in these early stages the group will be feeling its way, so everything must be done to put participants at their ease. From first to last Kingdom building on the estate is about relationships, and these foundational meetings should set the tone for the development of the *koinonia* solidarity that will become the essence of mature Kingdom living – where we grow together as the Body of Christ in that place.

The welcome stranger

There will be others too from outside the group who perhaps not being poor themselves will nevertheless have sensed a vocation to be among us on the poor estates. Many reading this book may well be in this category and will be wanting to find ways to do that well. Others will want to find some way of following the Kingdom values, but are not free to take such a radical step as actually joining a poor community. Each of us must respond to Jesus' Beatitudes as the limitations of our life allow, but we rejoice that of late the Church has seen a blossoming of preparedness, especially among the young, to embrace the challenge full on and commit to living with and alongside the poor for a concerted period. But for all of us the journey must be undertaken with great care and seriousness. It was John Vincent, the man who introduced the term 'Urban Theology' to the UK, who has written extensively about the 'journey downwards' (2004, Chapter 20). Having given up the possibility of a professorial career, he went to live with the poor in Sheffield and has since invited hundreds to join him for periods of their lives to do their theology there. He speaks of discipleship being a matter of following Jesus on a socially downward trajectory, so that they can best live out the full character of the Kingdom community and learn the deeper treasures of the faith as they go. It is important that we should all get as close as we can to this for as long as we are able, and continue always to hold fast to what we learn by doing so. But for those who undertake this journey there are cardinal rules that must be followed.

John Hayes (2007) has reminded us that in order to serve, the first action of the Good Samaritan was to get off his donkey so as to become fully engaged with the man who had fallen among thieves. This incarnational getting down to earth, this getting off our high horse, has been central to all that we've learned through this study and is one of the cardinal Kingdom values we see in Jesus' life with the poor. The Baptist Union Estates Group observed: 'Estate Churches do not wish to be patronized or swamped by middle class enthusiasm and competences. They would very much like to be befriended and respected' (Baptist Union of Great Britain 2000, p. 12). If we come in this way to listen and learn, we will hear what may at first sound like pointless chatter, but once we have our ear tuned to the wavelength, we will perceive that those conversations are telling us at least three very important things. That first, for the poor, life is essentially a relentless struggle; second, that everything on the estate has to do with relationships; and third, that to have faith in the future calls for great resilience. These three things alone, if heard at depth, will help the newcomer learn a great deal that will make sense of what they may meet later.

If on the other hand the incomer should unconsciously adopt a superior attitude, either because of upbringing or by virtue of being the designated and ordained 'leader', they may be greeted with either deferential subservience or hidden resentment – or both. Some domineering clergy nevertheless manage to organize everything and put on a successful show – but show is all that it is. One parish recently made it very clear that having had a time of vacancy – with no parish priest to serve them – they preferred to remain that way, suspecting that a newcomer would no longer let them continue with every member playing their part. For let us be clear, 'ministry' is the responsibility of every baptized Christian, and only when we have all truly understood this, does the ordained newcomer become the asset they are intended to be.

Total immersion

We're sometimes apt to think of Jesus as beginning his ministry as a young man, until we remember that the average male life-span in his day was probably around 26 years. He had therefore spent a lifetime deeply immersed in his context before he began his ministry. So it is today that those who have lived in a community all their lives will be the best companions to the welcome stranger, as together they walk the streets of the community looking and listening to their stories and the locals' understandings of their patch. It may take some years before the newcomer begins to feel at home as they walk, look, wander, listen, meet, chat, smell, feel and gently warm to the area and its people. They will then understand what has made a barren space into what local people own as their treasured place, and begin to treasure it themselves.

But if the poor are to claim their inheritance as the blessed of the Kingdom, they themselves must become more consciously aware of all this too. A parish in Basildon discovered an archive of old community photographs, which they displayed in the church over many weeks and invited local people in to unravel the history which was prompted by the pictures. Another group drew their own freehand map of the locality and its amenities to see what areas they considered important to the community's life and those parts that they scarcely knew about. Some local councillors were also able to tell the group the story of the political decisions and key people who had influenced the estate over the years, as the group unearthed the deeper causes of why their estate was the way it was. And a new consciousness began to arise as they delved into the facts about the local ethnic mix, the numbers in work or receiving benefits, the health and educational attainments, and so on. Suddenly the stories the community were apt to tell one another about the place were found not always to stand up to scrutiny.

As they discover more, some groups will become so taken by a particular facet of estate life that they want to hear what the researchers have written in reports such as the nationally acclaimed Hills Report on social housing (Hills 2007) or join campaigns such as Quaker Social Action or Faith in Affordable Housing. Masses of relevant data and all the links they need are readily available on line and especially from the Church Urban Fund.

And it will be crucial that the Christian group do all this exploration while keeping in touch with the people, the organizations and the other churches on their estates, so that they are constantly informed by the distinctive culture of their own community. All the time they must be 'reading' their own local culture, observing the clothing, listening to the language and the preferred music, hearing what the aspirations are of local people and what they do with their time; listening to any expressions or vestiges of faith that might crop up and chatting with friends to find out what local people really think about their churches.[2]

Groups who work their way through such a process of discovery together can find it all very affirming, for it enables them to speak with real authority about their estate. And as this work progresses, so previously hidden gifts in the group emerge too. Some will have gifts as creators of group cohesion, others will be ferreters after facts and figures, some will have become the helpfully critical voices, some quiet but staunch and supportive, while still others are able to hold their own in the face of opposition. Hopefully, even those who tended to rule the roost or previously voiced racist or hide-bound views will have become more open and inclusive and more integrated into the group as others have found a voice and their gifts too have been affirmed.

Pavement-level theology

Once the group has this assured appreciation of its context it is able to bring its experience of its estate into a much deeper relationship with its maturing Christian faith by using all the tools

2 Chapter 4 of my *Let's Do Theology* describes the many ways that there are of unearthing the data, while Benny Hazlehurst and Chris Chapman have produced a four-part *Do It Yourself Estate Kit*, which takes an estate group through some of these processes (2002).

of theological reflection that I have already described very thoroughly in *Let's Do Theology*. The foregoing chapters of this study have given numerous examples of the insights that may come to light when the poor use these tools and bring their contextual perspective to bear upon the Bible and the doctrines of the faith, but every estate group will find new treasures for themselves. I do want to take a moment, however, to illustrate how powerful this process can be by noting the work of one of our estate groups in Sheffield.

Realizing that many of the hymns and prayers in our set liturgies do not really resonate with our housing estate experience, the group began to study the biblical book of Lamentations. Many of these Lamentations derive from the pain of exile – a theme we have already touched on as having strong resonance with our housing estate experiences. The Lamentations follow a particular structure – first they address God, then each Lamentation describes the people's troubles, then they implore God to attend to their struggling community, and finally, rather than assuming that God will sort it all out for them, the Lamentation ends with a faithful salutation that acknowledges God's presence with them. The Sheffield group felt these biblical writers had created a form of prayer that did justice to the sort of struggles being experienced on their estates, and so they began to write their own lamentations. The following is one of many.[3]

My God, the One whose face I seek every morning.
Why do you allow all this pain to cycle round for people?
I see a lot, but you must see it all.
The low self-esteem, bad decisions about relationships, bad decisions about money.
About everything.
How are people supposed to make good decisions
With all the odds stacked against them?
Turn! Pay attention to the people of this estate.

3 See Julie Upton's report in the NECN's Summer 2014 newsletter at www.nationalestatechurches.org.

Hear their cries of despair and pain.
These people were made in your image,
You say you love them, know every hair on their heads.
You said you knew them before they were born!
How will they know your love unless you hear their cries?
Destroy the Evil One who tempts people with rubbish they can't afford
And into relationships with violent people.
Make the plans of violent and selfish people turn to dust.
God, you are our God.
People of God, know his power to hear, to save, to rescue us from despair and death.

This is a powerful example of how, knowing their estate well, their theological reflection on the Lamentations has freed the group to articulate some key issues and to focus the mismatch between the estate's predicament and the Kingdom they yearn for. In doing so, they have found a form of prayer more apposite than those they have received from elsewhere. Furthermore, they have voiced very powerfully the injustice inherent in their situation, so that their theological reflection can then propel them forward, ready for action.

We have learned that the poor can be just as much at the mercy of society's prevailing myths as anyone else, and it is not at all unusual for poor people to become quite heated in their criticism of the 'undeserving' poor or those from differing ethnicities. But taking part in the process of exploration and theological reflection can often elicit a very evident change of heart and mind. 'I thought it was just us who didn't get their fair share,' Alice admitted, 'but we got all the facts, and then read the story about the labourers in the vineyard. I began to think p'raps it's all of us in the same mess – waiting around for jobs. Just 'cos they've arrived later than us is no reason to think they've got it any easier, is it? I hadn't thought of it like that before.' It is reassuring that by following the process we have utilized throughout this study, an estate group can often be liberated from previously held oppressive opinions, by reflecting on matters from the perspective of the Kingdom and realizing how their own pain has been projected on to others who are suffering the self-same oppression. Emil Cioran had his own way of putting it: 'Great persecutors are recruited among martyrs whose heads haven't been cut off.'

Radical educators have called this process 'conscientization' – bringing to consciousness the truths about our predicament that were previously hidden from us by the myths, prejudices and projections of the culture that surrounds us.[4] We might equally call it 'bringing sight to the blind'. We saw this happening when we learned for example that while on the surface the poor appear to be the ones benefiting from the credits that top up their poor wages, when we asked who was truly benefiting we observed that the employer who pays substandard wages is benefiting most of all. Increases in the housing benefit budget was similarly discovered to be benefiting those landlords who are increasing their rents unfairly. Asking who is benefiting most from any situation is a sure-fire way of uncovering the hidden truths of oppressive structures and is constantly used as a tool in the process of conscientization. In addition to asking who really benefits, we can also get under evil's radar by noting that the deception often hides itself in a simple statement. But if we transform the statement into a question we are then brought up sharp, able to see the injustice for what it is. For example, if the statement that many poor people live on our estates is transformed into the question 'Why do so many poor people live on our estates?', we have immediately unmasked a problem and we are on course for conscientization. The words of the martyr Archbishop Hélder Câmara come to mind: 'When I feed the poor, people call me a saint, but if I ask why they are poor, they brand me a communist.'

In our small local groups, theological reflection acts in this same way, by 'unmasking the powers', as we saw in our reflection on the Lord's Prayer. From the context of the group will come issues

4 The clearest description of the conscientization process appears in Paulo Freire's book *Pedagogy of the Oppressed* (1972). It was tremendously influential in the UK for those of us who were developing contextual theological methodology.

of housing, poverty, alienation, demonization, hunger and lots more, and these will be the springboard for prayerful reflection upon the truths of our faith so that the issues of injustice become clear and the values of the Kingdom shine ever more powerfully. And once this awareness is aroused we can do no other than respond with action to see Kingdom values prevail.

A people of action

Churches that make their decisions on the basis not of the Kingdom values, but instead on business or cultural expectations, do some rather bizarre things. I know one parish church that expends much energy organizing an annual pre-Christmas shopping visit to New York with a Broadway show thrown in. Quite why, nobody asks. Some denominations have closed down thriving missional programmes on financial grounds alone. We might call this Christendom rather than Kingdom decision-making. The latter issues from attentive listening to what the Spirit has to say to the Churches through the mediation of the poor, just as we have been seeking to do in our study. And such listening can produce Kingdom action in the most unlikely places, even in very affluent congregations. In one such church the congregation had assembled to welcome its new minister, when an extremely scruffy, not to say smelly, man came in off the street at the back of the church. During the first hymn, he went from pew to pew asking for a hand-out and received some very dusty responses. When the new pastor was invited to come forward, it was revealed that he had just returned from a month on retreat, where he had been praying about the wealth of his new congregation and the poverty of the area in which it met. He had therefore resolved that for the remainder of his retreat he would live on the streets with the poor. So their new pastor was none other than their unwelcomed smelly visitor. He came forward to explain himself – but his point had already been made, provocatively and prophetically. He had sought to respond to a situation of grave injustice while signalling what Kingdom life could entail.

Some congregations have thrown themselves into frenetic activity in the belief that action of itself demonstrates a Kingdom orientation, but we must take care about filling our lives with projects, because such programmes can easily become rather self-gratifying, focusing upon our own abilities and managerial prowess rather than pointing to the Kingdom. Projects have also been known to become excuses for the rest of the congregation to rest on their laurels and point to the church project as if it were proof of their own personal engagement. Some churches are so full of rather churchy projects that congregational members have no energy left to engage with others in the community for the common good.

But for all that, many fine projects, resulting from careful theological reflection and prayer, target issues and speak volumes about Kingdom values. One Bradford initiative called 'Powerful Whispers' was designed in just this way and issued in bringing together housing developers and their estate tenants. Each group was asked to listen intently and without interruption to the other's differing interpretation of a recent consultation process. Elaine Appelbee helped to lead the initiative and describes (2003, p. 164) how the developers were truly astonished to realize that what they had assumed to have been their very successful 'bottom up' consultation had actually involved them in very little listening but a great deal of telling. It was a simple project but from it came a new determination for the participants to work together for the benefit of all – choosing as their template for analysis and future action nothing other than the words of the Magnificat – the song of Mary.

Another congregation began by reflecting on the biblical stories of creation and on Jesus' parables about growth, and on looking at their estate environment and the diets of local tenants, responded by turning over their churchyard to a community allotment club. Some groups have chosen to do this hand in hand with their local schools and community organizations. The Chepstow Community Garden brings a wide variety of people together who otherwise would regard one another with suspicion, to enjoy healthy natural activity right in the heart of what is otherwise a concrete jungle. Of course, some of these projects have not been initiated by Christian groups, but Christians have felt themselves called to support them because of the Kingdom qualities they see there. This has the advantage of making sure that we put ourselves alongside others on their own terms, affirming and serving. It is more apostolic too, in that when the Church supports the local initiatives of others, it is moving out into the community rather than taking a stand at the centre and expecting others to come to it.

Debt is a key issue in the Lord's Prayer, as we've recognized, and many churches have responded to that insight by opening credit unions on their premises. In the Beulah Baptist Church, in addition to the credit union on Fridays, debt and money management counselling and mentoring is also provided by a small team of specialists, who have been brought in by the estate church. The local pay-day loan shops and the betting shop still attract far more customers, but already many families have had their lives turned around and, although still finding life difficult, are no longer living in fear of debt.

In similar vein, many Christians aware of the hunger around them have volunteered to help at foodbanks only to realize that an inspired project like that does more than might originally have been intended. Having met and got to know recipients their eyes are opened to deeper truths about our society. This is why Bishop Tim Thornton teamed up with Frank Field MP to produce the cross-party parliamentary report on Hunger and Food Poverty in Britain using evidence from the foodbanks to call for important changes in society.[5] In this way, good projects will often give Christian groups opportunity to serve, to alleviate suffering or bring enjoyment to the community, but they will also placard injustices back to society and inspire real change that is both personal and political. To further this objective it is helpful when groups take care to inform their bishop or sponsoring network about their projects and to use the web and social media so that the deeper significance of what is happening can be signalled more widely to influence change. But if our projects are truly to be signs

5 See www.foodpovertyinquiry.org.

of God's Kingdom in this way, our congregations must be sure to engage in prayer and in theological action–reflection before, during and after each and every one, to ensure that our projects truly are those thin places – sacraments of the Kingdom. A project that is simply an end in itself will not be pointing to the Kingdom, but will rather be prompting that critical question: who is it then who is actually benefiting?

Finally, we need to be open to the possibility that our theological reflection will teach us that a project would not be the right thing at all in the circumstances. We might be led to realize that we have been overwhelming our lives with so much activity based on our own church's needs that we are in danger of losing sight of God's agenda. This process can therefore lead some groups to cut back on activity, so that their prayer and spiritual life may first deepen. It might be of course that their age or limited resources quite lend themselves to being simply a steady presence in an otherwise chaotic estate. One young group has come to the same conclusion and like to call their response 'Hanging Out Ministry' – simply being there with people on the streets and in the communal areas of the estate, making friends and perhaps in time encouraging more meaningful conversation. At the Newcastle Cornerstone they pride themselves on providing simply a welcoming space, where anyone can drop in and find companionship. They are then happy to put their visitors in touch with the helping agencies, while they themselves offer a safe space, a sanctuary. A very wise monk, Father Michael Casey, has called his book *An Unexciting Life* (2005), and that title is a pointed challenge to over-active churches. Most lives are not glamorous nor overtly exciting, and for a very poor family excitement may be a false answer to their deepest needs. Many estate congregations are hanging on by a thread just like so many around them. These fragile churches are very special in that they truly represent the people of the area, but it means that the congregational members will probably not have the energy to engage in programmes or projects at all – maybe not even managing to keep the glass mended in their church windows. But as Michael Casey's book, which is about Kingdom sanctity, makes clear, sometimes the most unexciting life can be very close indeed to the mystery of God and will have much to teach glitzy evangelism.

Holistic mission

I have been particularly heartened to find that the old church divide between social engagement work and making disciples is at last breaking down. There will always remain the tension in mission between assimilation and distinctiveness, between being embedded in the local culture and yet being committed to an alternative Kingdom – being in the world and yet not of it – but where this tension is dynamic and not defensive it is proving to be extraordinarily creative.

Patton Taylor is Professor of Old Testament and Principal Emeritus of Union Theological College in Belfast, but won his spurs in the Antrim Road district during the troubles. He tells how his Protestant church sought to minister to the Catholic young people of the surrounding area and came to grief, not because of the denominational divide, but, as one youngster put it, 'These kids don't really care about any of that. The real barrier between you and the kids is that you're all so middle class and affluent. You come in from outside and you don't know what it's like to live around here.' Patton explains that the decision was therefore made to move to a style much more in line with what we have been led to in this study – an incarnational, listening and socially concerned Kingdom ministry – a journey downwards. Patton tells us that they stopped bringing mission teams in for

> a hit and run raid of evangelism each summer, for we needed Christians permanently living in the community . . . We have learned that paradoxically we have more influence now that we have less control . . . Our desire to share the gospel is undiminished; but staff now do so primarily by working alongside local people and taking opportunities to share their faith informally . . . God has led us along the community development road in which it is the living out of 'Kingdom values' that gives

> us the opportunity to speak of the eternal Good News (Taylor 2004, pp. 97–9).

Francis of Assisi said essentially the same thing when he famously remarked to his followers: 'Preach the gospel at every opportunity. Use words only if necessary.'

In the Blackpool area, the Grange Park Open Door provides fine breakfasts at very reasonable cost, and the ecumenical volunteers meet half an hour beforehand to say their prayers and discuss the faith. Surprise, surprise – many locals who ostensibly come just for the food are in the habit of arriving early and sitting at the edges of the room, silently soaking it in, knowing that they will not be pressured. They say they are just there for the breakfast and the chat, but why then do they habitually come so early and listen so intently? Most, of course, arrive after the prayers and are served their breakfast and enjoy the warm and friendly atmosphere – and that too is a fine sign of the Kingdom.

In Leicester, when I asked the people of Braunstone Estate Church what their guiding intention for mission was, they told me it was threefold: empowerment, being a serving community, and making new disciples. Furthermore, the three were to their mind intricately interwoven, and they were adamant that making new disciples meant something more than merely increasing the number in the congregation, but rather deepening the faith of those already there and empowering them and others for an outward Kingdom life. The Church Urban Fund undertakes painstaking research, and one of their reports has unearthed some intriguing facts about growing churches. They asked some 900 Anglican clergy to report on their parishes and found that most felt that 'tackling poverty locally contributes to a more outward-looking church, a deeper understanding of God's purpose and improved relations within the church and with the wider community, and *they are also more likely to be growing*. This confirms the findings from our qualitative research' (Church Urban Fund 2012b). When Christians engage alongside others in Kingdom activity, people sense the integrity of the mission, they see it, perhaps begin to feel the presence, and want to know more.

Many years as parish priest in the Holme Wood Estate in Bradford had taught Gordon Dey that if a parish were simply to model itself on the many facets of Jesus' ministry, a healthy church would result. He therefore encouraged very mixed groups to work out for themselves what those ministry components might have been. Their list enumerated five major elements: Jesus responded to the needs of people, especially people who were on the edge; he used everyday language for story-based teaching that was challenging but not condemning; he spent quality time away with the Disciples for their own development; he maintained his own spiritual life as essential; and was often in conflict with the authorities, because he shone a searchlight of truth into those corners they kept covered. Having agreed through their biblical reflection that these priorities were evident in Jesus' ministry style, the parish then did its best to conform its life and conduct to those priorities. It worked so well that the idea was rolled out to other estate churches all around and has become known as the Jesus Shaped People programme (Dey 2014). The evaluation report says that the little churches are growing, there's a greater commitment to prayer, they feel more engaged in the worship, are involved with the needs of the community, and they generally feel more alive and vibrant. There is a blessing in discovering that they are themselves a blessing to one another and can be a blessing to their community – the poor, blessed indeed.

Juliet Kilpin of Urban Expression also presses for us to follow Jesus' incarnational example. Therefore she is keen to advise those contemplating coming in from outside the estate to work always with the indigenous local church congregation wherever possible rather than setting up as if in opposition, ignoring what the local poor have to teach us, and imposing our own prejudices and styles upon the vulnerable (Kilpin and Murray 2007). John Hayes, living on the same estate, takes his lead once again from the story of the Good Samaritan:

> If from our living alongside the poor for some years, someone wants to become a Christian, we take them along with us to our local denominational church, and only if the Inn won't take them in do we contemplate the thought that we might have to set up a separate plant.

I was therefore disappointed to see recently a notice about the arrival of a new plant in an estate that I had only just visited. I contacted them immediately to let them know that there was already a thriving congregation on that estate and that it was really reaching out into the community. My heart sank when they told me that even by this late stage in their planning they knew nothing about it. What's more they could not understand why the indigenous church felt so diminished and upset by their project, and they went ahead regardless. Church planting can be a wonderful missional project, but it does call for extraordinary sensitivity and is best done in the company of those who already have a track record of embedded incarnational ministry if the new arrivals are to learn Kingdom lessons from the poor.

There are certainly some glorious examples of where a new experiment of what it is to be Church has really caught the imagination of local people who have taken it to their heart and made it their own. The Terminus Café in Sheffield was celebrating its tenth anniversary when I popped in to visit. It is sponsored by a small ecumenical team from the local church and is situated by the bus terminus in one of the small row of shops as a drop-in café. Its launch was handled so well that over the years the locals have made it their own. They themselves now have a befriending service, the local health workers use it as a base, there are groups for mutual support, and lots of things for children too. Joy Adams and Harry Steele are quite upfront about it being a Christian project, but in a very relaxed and sensitive way – and the Muslim shopkeeper at the newsagent said that it doesn't feel like Christmas to him until the Café have sung their carols each year.

But there are many challenges in steering a course of holistic ministry, so that we do not allow our Christian identity to be overwhelmed by our immersion in the community, nor our life to be so church-centred that we are no longer integral to the life of our estate. The answer is to bring both together in the theological reflection group, so that our faith and our context are always held in creative tension, each informing the other in Kingdom living. This theologically contextual style is one of the poor's greatest gifts to the Churches.

Worship – foretaste of the Kingdom

Worship is humankind's highest endeavour and is itself a foretaste of the Kingdom, but given the very meagre resources of our estate churches, our worship can sometimes feel somewhat lacking. We should therefore not forget that worship is not just something we offer to God, but it is also a place where God takes us and transforms us, and as we've been learning, this can happen in the most unlikely of settings. Just before the Orthodox service begins, the deacon whispers in the ear of the priest, 'Be alert – God is about to act!', and it is that action, not our polished performance, that is the heart of good worship.

Our difficulty is that the Christendom Church has saddled itself with liturgy that is too dependent on text, long concentration spans and top-down leadership, and which is not, as Cranmer the compiler of the first English service book said it should be, 'understanded of the people'.[6] There is so much off-the-shelf material of quality available today, including DVDs, worship outlines and so on, but nothing can beat the home-grown service for authenticity and engagement. As Ann Morisy has explained (Morisy 2004), estate worship must be 'apt', connecting with the issues that matter here and now to the worshippers, and be appropriate to their needs and gifts. But we must also recognize that worship that is limited only to the local can miss out on the wonder and mystery of being at one with the worshipping community through the ages and

6 Book of Common Prayer 1662, Preface.

around the world – it denies the poor congregation the catholicity which is their birth-right as baptized Christians. But the wordy and impenetrable liturgies on offer at present do not honour the poor as members of the Body of Christ, but if local congregations are enabled to bring their own concerns and weave those into simplified outlines of those universal liturgies, the ethos and style of the worship can become appropriate for the estate, enabling them to bring their best before God.

But more than anything, we have to be sure that whatever style is right for our place and our group, the structure and the content of the worship is grounded in our Kingdom values (NECN 2003). Tim Stratford has helpfully drawn our attention to how the doing theology cycle in some ways mirrors the process at the heart of all good estate worship (Stratford 2006). As always, we start from our experience – finding ways to bring the life of the estate and the particular anxieties, joys or sorrows of its people into the gathering. Kathy Galloway of the Iona Community once told me that she had a friend who had lived in a mining village all through the trauma of the great miners' strike and this totally overwhelmed and changed the community, but not once in all that time was it ever mentioned in the services at the village church. The realities of our lives and that of the estate community must be brought to our worship and symbolically presented there so that they can then be reflected in Bible readings, prayers and music so that the congregation can reflect upon how those readings throw light on their experience – a sermon or discussion gives opportunity for that to happen. When the service has brought together our heartfelt experiences and the treasures of Bible and liturgy, then comes that moment of transformation that is God's to give – often symbolized in sacrament, music or colour. For many that moment is particularly evident when sharing Communion. As Alf said, 'walking up to take Communion can be like stepping through the magic wardrobe – it's a place where heaven and earth seem to meet'. If this transformation by God is really owned, it will lead directly to the participants knowing that they need to make a response, and the worship must allow for that before ending with a commitment of ourselves to one another, to our community and to the God who sends us out in solidarity to serve the world.

When our worship follows this pattern, which is both the pattern of the 'doing theology' cycle and the essence of traditional worship through the centuries, then it holds before God all that we have sought to do through the chapters of this book. It will have taken our experience of the poor housing estate seriously, wrapping it in prayer and exploration, it will have opened it to the transforming power of God and then helped us to respond with our deepest commitment, so that we might see those glimpses of the Kingdom of God.

Conclusion: Blessed are You who are Poor

When I first set out on this study, I felt anxious about the task, because the culture that seems to be engulfing us at present is very antagonistic to thinking about the poor in anything but negative terms. They are derided, ridiculed and blamed for all the ills of our society, even if Jesus pronounces them blessed. However, as I began to investigate the matter, it became evident that this was no new phenomenon and that through history the poor have always been despised and excluded. It was as difficult to hear Jesus' words when he first spoke them as it is today. And through the generations biblical commentators and preachers have therefore gone to great lengths in seeking, against all the odds, to prove that Jesus did not really mean it when he announced: 'Blessed are you who are poor.' But it has been the poor themselves who have given me the privilege of being alongside them and learning something of Jesus' meaning, and I see now that those commentators were simply as scared as most of us are when facing up to the Kingdom challenges with which Jesus presents us. He challenges us as individuals, and he challenges us as Church, to turn and have a new mind, a mind open to the fact that he placed the poor at the vanguard of the Kingdom, and it has been an extraordinary loss to the Church that we have subsequently ignored what they therefore have to teach us.

In the past, we have seen the poor only as those for whom we should have an especial care, ministering to them in their need and seeking to alleviate the injustices attendant upon their poverty. Others have argued that such a Social Gospel approach fails to appreciate a deeper need for the poor to hear the saving message of the Good News so that their lives may no longer be starved of that most costly treasure. It may very well be that these two understandings have some merit, but they have too often been offered to those at the margins of society as if they were the magnanimous largess of the comfortable. But Jesus has pulled the rug from under this assumption of superiority by telling us that in his Kingdom it is the poor who are at the centre, and it is the rich who are so much on its margins that they are the ones in danger of falling off.

When at last the Kingdom of God is realized, the concern of those who are not poor will then become not how to include the poor, but whether or not the poor will have the grace to include them. In the parable of Dives and Lazarus, the rich man laments that his conversion to this realization has come all too late, when he learns that 'between us and you a great gulf has been fixed, to prevent those who want to cross from our side to yours or from your side to ours' (Luke 16.26). In this study, we have sought to destroy the gulf in our Church between rich and poor, that we might all share in God's inclusive Kingdom, but we have learned that very grave changes will be required of us all if we are to accomplish that task. The whole Church will have to place itself alongside the poor and begin to learn afresh from them about the demands and the rewards of Kingdom living.

In Luke 9.23–26, we hear Jesus telling us that following him will demand that we lose our lives for his sake that we might save them: 'What benefit is it to anyone to win the whole world and forfeit or lose his very self? For if anyone is ashamed of me and of my words, of him the Son of man will be ashamed . . . ' We have been listening very closely to the words of Jesus and realizing that the poor teach us all this very thing – that by seeking gain we lose the very thing for which we most yearn, and that poverty is in fact the proper estimation of ourselves as we draw closer to God, as Aquinas taught us. We do not merit God's attention because of our success but by our vulnerable humanity, and only on that basis, alongside the poor, should we present ourselves before God. If we can become thus 'poor in spirit', the Son of man will no longer be ashamed of us, but will see the image of God welling up in us, releasing in us all the gifts, talents and graces with which he originally endowed us. But this can only be learned from the poor, who are way ahead of us on the road to the Kingdom. In their company, we all learn together how injustice can be solved by radical inclusion and mutual generosity, for once we have owned the truth of our interconnectedness, then we can fight together for the eradication of the imposed poverty which demeans, divides and disfigures. It is a call to cultural reformation in the Church and in society, that 'Every valley shall be lifted up, and every mountain and hill be made low' (Isa. 40.4, RSV). But we will not be able to engage in this cultural battle with any integrity or clear direction unless those who now live in those valleys of poverty are brought to the centre of our attention, understanding and reverence.

The people of our poorer housing estates must not be forgotten. They offer us all, supremely, the perspective from which to see the truth about our society. The millions of poor people around the world should not be forgotten, because God does not forget them; he teaches us to learn many things from them, and he asks them to play a privileged part in the drama of the Kingdom. And that is why he looks so concertedly towards them and pronounces 'Blessed are you who are poor'.

Bibliography

Aldrete, Gregory S., 2004, *Daily Life in Roman Britain: Rome, Pompeii and Ostia*, Norman, OK: University of Oklahoma Press.

Aldridge, Hannah, *et al.*, 2012, *Monitoring Poverty and Social Exclusion*, York: Joseph Rowntree Foundation.

Anderson, Gary A., 2013, *Charity: The Place of the Poor in the Biblical Tradition*, New Haven: Yale University Press.

Appelbee, Elaine, 2003, 'Shaping a Changing Society', in Vincent, J. J. (ed.), 2003, *Faithfulness in the City*, Hawarden: Monad Press, p. 164.

Baker, David, 2001, *Looking into the Future: Evangelical Studies in Eschatology*, Evangelical Theological Society Studies, Grand Rapids: Baker Academic Press.

Bamfield, Louise, and Horton, Tim, 2009, *Understanding Attitudes to Tackling Economic Inequality*, York: Joseph Rowntree Foundation.

Baptist Union of Great Britain, Estates Group, 2000, *Estate Gospel Agents*.

Baptist Union of Great Britain, with Methodist Church, Church of Scotland and United Reformed Church, 2013, *The Lies We Tell Ourselves: Ending Comfortable Myths about Poverty*, a report.

Barrett, Al, 2013, *Asset-Based Community Development: A Theological Reflection*, London, CUF.

Barrett, Al, and Delmege, Andy, 2011, *Strengthening Estate Ministry – Thriving in Mission*, Birmingham: Birmingham Diocese.

Barth, Karl, 1963, *Evangelical Theology: An Introduction*, New York: Holt, Rinehart & Winston.

BBC, 2012, 'The Growing Demand for Food Banks in Breadline Britain', BBC Newsnight Blog, http://www.bbc.co.uk/news/uk-19468697.

Becker, Ulrich, 1975, 'Blessing – *Makarios*', in Colin Brown (ed.), *The New International Dictionary of New Testament Theology, Vol. 1*, Exeter: Paternoster Press, p. 217.

Big Issue, 16 July 2012, p. 19.

Blackburn, Simon, 2014, *Mirror, Mirror: The Uses and Abuses of Self-love*, Princeton: Princeton University Press.

Bochenski, Michael, 2000, *Sent into All the World: Good News for the Housing Estates of Britain – a Journal*, published by the author.

Boerma, Conrad, 1979, *Rich Man, Poor Man – and the Bible*, London: SCM Press.

Bonino, José Míguez, 1983, *Toward a Christian Political Ethics*, London: SCM Press.

Boring, M. Eugene, 1995, in *The New Interpreter's Bible, Vol. VIII*, Nashville: Abingdon Press, p. 206.

Brown, Colin (ed.), 1975, *The New International Dictionary of New Testament Theology, Vol. 1*, Exeter: Paternoster Press.

Brown, Wallace and Mary, undated, *The Hidden Poor*, Report to the Diocese of Birmingham.

Browne, James, and Hood, Andrew, 2012, *A Survey of the UK Benefit System*, London: Institute for Fiscal Studies.

Casey, Michael, 2005, *An Unexciting Life: Reflections on Benedictine Life*, Petersham, MA: St Bede's Publications.

Charlesworth, Martin, and Williams, Natalie, 2014, *The Myth of the Undeserving Poor: A Christian Response to Poverty in Britain Today, 2014*, Guildford: Jubilee Plus Ltd, and Guildford: Grosvenor House Publishing Ltd.

Church Urban Fund, 2011, 'Area-Based Poverty', *Church Urban Fund Research Papers*.

Church Urban Fund, 2012a, 'Bias to the Poor?', *Church Urban Fund Research Papers*.

Church Urban Fund, 2012b, 'Growing Church Through Social Action: A National Survey of Church-based Action to Tackle Poverty'.

Coles, Bob, *et al.*, 1998, *Working with Young People on Estates: The Role of Housing Professionals in Multi-agency Work*, York and Coventry: Joseph Rowntree Foundation and The Chartered Institute of Housing.

Crossan, John Dominic, 1992, *The Historical Jesus: The Life of a Mediterranean Peasant*, New York: HarperCollins, Part II, 'Brokerless Kingdom'.

Crossan, John Dominic, 1995, *Jesus: A Revolutionary Biography*, San Francisco: HarperCollins.

D'Angelo, Mary Rose, 1992, 'Abba and "Father": Imperial Theology and the Jesus Tradition', *Journal of Biblical Literature*, 3.4, Winter 1992, pp. 611–30.

Dey, Gordon, 2014, *Jesus Shaped People*, www.jesusshapedpeople.net.

Engels, Friedrich, *The Condition of the Working-Class in England in 1844*, www.gutenberg.org.

Field, Frank, and Thompson, Timothy (eds), 2014, *Feeding Britain: A Strategy for Zero Hunger in England, Wales, Scotland and Northern Ireland*, London: Children's Society.

Fitzpatrick, Suzanne, and Stephens, Mark (eds), 2009, *The Future of Social Housing*, London: Shelter.

Franks, Christopher, 2009, *He Became Poor: The Poverty of Christ and Aquinas' Economic Teachings*, Grand Rapids: Eerdmans.

Freire, Paulo, 1972, *Pedagogy of the Oppressed*, Harmondsworth: Penguin Books.

Gomory, Ralph, and Sylla, Richard, 2013, 'The American Corporation', *Daedalus*, 142.2, pp. 102–18.

Government, 2000, *Our Towns and Cities – the Future: Urban White Paper*, November 2000, Office of the Deputy Prime Minister.

Government, 2003, *Full Employment in Every Region*, HM Treasury and Department of Work and Pensions, London: TSO.

Government, 2010, *Tackling Fraud and Error in the Welfare System*, HMRC/DWP (online version now corrected).

Government, 2012, *Local Authority Breakdown: Incapacity Benefits and Disability Living Allowance Claimants with Main Condition of Alcohol or Drug Abuse*, July 2012, Department of Work and Pensions Ad-hoc analysis.

Government, 2013, *Social Security Benefits and Expenditure*, January 2013, House of Commons Library paper SN/SG/2656.

Green, Laurie, 1987, *Power to the Powerless: Theology Brought to Life*, Basingstoke: Marshall Pickering.

Green, Laurie, 1990, *Let's Do Theology: A Pastoral Cycle Resource Book*, London: Mowbray.

Green, Laurie, 1995, 'The Body: Physicality in the UPA', in Peter Sedgwick (ed.), *God in the City: Essays and Reflections from the Archbishop of Canterbury's Urban Theology Group*, London: Mowbray, pp. 105ff.

Green, Laurie, 1997, *Jesus and the Jubilee: The Kingdom of God and Our New Millennium*, London and Sheffield: Jubilee 2000 and UTU Press, New City Special No. 11.

Green, Laurie, 2000, *The Challenge of the Estates: Strategies and Theology for Housing Estate Ministry*, London: Urban Bishops' Panel and NECN Press.

Green, Laurie, 2003, *Urban Ministry and the Kingdom of God*, London: SPCK.

Green, Laurie, 2009, *Let's Do Theology: Resources for Contextual Theology*, London: Mowbray.

Green, Laurie, 2013, 'Liberation Theology and Urban Theology', in Rowland, Chris, and Vincent, John (eds), *British Liberation Theology – For Church and Nation*, Sheffield: Urban Theology Unit.

Green, Laurie, and Baker, Chris (eds), 2008, *Building Utopia? Seeking the Authentic Church for New Communities*, London: SPCK.

Grindrod, John, 2013, *Concretopia: A Journey Around the Rebuilding of Postwar Britain*, Brecon: Old Street Publishing.

Hanley, Lynsey, 2007, *The Estates: An Intimate History*, London: Granta Books.

Harvey, A. E., 1990, *Strenuous Commands: The Ethics of Jesus*, London: SCM Press.

Harvey, A. E., 2004, *A Companion to the New Testament*, Cambridge: Cambridge University Press.

Hasler, Joe, 2006, *Crying Out for a Polycentric Church: Christ Centred and Culturally Focused Congregations*, Maidstone: Church in Society.

Hayes, John, 2007, *Sub-merge: Living Deep in a Shallow World*, Delight, AR: Gospel Light Publications.

Hazlehurst, Benny, and Chapman, Chris, 2002, *Do It Yourself Estate Kit*, London: Southwark Anglican Diocese for NECN.

Herzog, William, R., II, 1999, *Jesus, Justice and the Reign of God: A Ministry of Liberation*, Louisville: Westminster John Knox Press.

Hills, John, 2007, *Ends and Means: The Future Roles of Social Housing in England*, CASE Report 34, London: ESRC Research Centre for Analysis and Social Exclusion (CASE), London School of Economics.

Hirst, Michael, 2012, 'Location, Location, Location', *Methodist Recorder*, 10 May 2012, p. 8.

Jones, Colin, and Murie, Alan, 2006, *The Right to Buy: Analysis and Evaluation of Housing Policy*, Oxford: Blackwell.

Juvenal, cited in Worth, R. H., 1999, *The Seven Cities of the Apocalypse and Roman Culture*, Mahwah: Paulist Press, p. 41.

Keeble, Paul, 2004, 'Gang Violence', in Eastman, Michael, and Latham, Steve (eds), 2004, *Urban Church: A Practitioner's Resource Book*, London: SPCK.

Kilpin, Juliet, and Murray, Stuart (now Stuart Murray Williams), 2007, *Church Planting in the Inner City*, Cambridge: Grove Booklets.

Lockwood, Trevor, 1993, *The Church on the Housing Estate: Mission and Ministry on the Urban Estate*, London: Methodist Church Home Mission.

Lupton, Ruth, *et al.*, 2009, *Growing Up in Social Housing in Britain: A Profile of Four Generations from 1946 to the Present Day*, London: Tenant Services Authority, and York: Joseph Rowntree Foundation.

May, Don, and Simey, Margaret, 1989, *The Servant Church in Granby*, Occasional Papers on Church and Society, Liverpool: Centre for Urban Studies.

McAfee Brown, Robert, 1979, 'Preface', in Gustavo Gutierrez, *The Power of the Poor in History*, London: SCM Press.

McCann, J. C. Jr, 1996, 'The Book of Psalms', *The New Interpreter's Bible, Vol. IV*, Nashville: Abingdon Press, p. 847.

McKenzie, Lisa, 2015, *Getting By: Estates, Class and Culture in Austerity Britain*, Bristol: The Policy Press.

Mealand, David, 1980, *Poverty and Expectation in the Gospels*, London: SPCK.

Morisy, Ann, 2004, *Journeying Out*, London: Continuum.

Mundle, W., 1975, 'Epiousios', in Brown, Colin (ed.), *The New International Dictionary of New Testament Theology, Vol. 1*, Exeter: Paternoster Press, p. 251.

Murray, Stuart (now Stuart Murray Williams), 2004, *Post-Christendom: Church and Mission in a Strange New World*, Carlisle: Paternoster Press.

Myers, Bryant, 2011, *Walking with the Poor: Principles and Practices of Transformational Development*, Maryknoll: Orbis.

Myers, Ched, 1998, *Binding the Strong Man: A Political Reading of Mark's Story of Jesus*, Maryknoll: Orbis.

NECN, 2003, *Worship for Housing Estate Ministry: Singing the Lord's Song in a Strange Land?*, from National Estate Churches Network.

Newman, Adrian, 2010, 'So Yesterday: Urban Ministry 25 Years on from *Faith in the City*', an unpublished sabbatical reflection.

Oxfam, 2012, *The Perfect Storm: Economic Stagnation, the Rising Cost of Living, Public Spending Cuts, and the Impact on UK Poverty*, London: Oxfam.

Pearson, Kate, 2014, 'I Dare You to Love Your Local Church', article originally published by Threads online magazine at www.threadsuk.com.

Pope Francis, 2013, *Apostolic Exhortation – Evangelii gaudium*, http://www.vatican.va/evangelii-gaudium/en/.

Pope Leo XIII, 1889, *Rerum novarum*, http://w2.vatican.va/content/leo-xiii/en/encyclicals/documents/hf_l-xiii_enc_15051891_rerum-novarum.html.

Power, Anne, 1999, *Estates on the Edge: The Social Consequences of Mass Housing in Northern Europe*, London: Macmillan Press.

Purnell, Derek, 2003, 'Urban Presence. Newton Heath, Manchester', in Vincent John, (ed.), *Faithfulness in the City*, Sheffield: Urban Theology Collective, Monad Press.

Raban, Jonathan, 1974, *Soft City*, London: Hamish Hamilton.

Rochester Diocese, 2015, *Challenging Poverty 2015*, at www.rochester.anglican.org.

Rodger, R., 1992, 'Scotland', in Pooley, C. G. (ed.), *Housing Strategies in Europe, 1880–1930*, Leicester: Leicester University Press.

Rubenstein, Jeffrey, 2003, *The Culture of the Babylonian Talmud*, Baltimore: Johns Hopkins University Press.

Sawicki, Marianne, 2000, *Crossing Galilee: Architectures of Contact in the Occupied Land of Jesus*, Harrisburg: Trinity Press International.

Sentamu, John, 2015, *On Rock or Sand? Firm Foundations for Britain's Future*, London: SPCK.

Sheppard, David, 1983, *Bias to the Poor*, London: Hodder & Stoughton.

Smith, Adam, 1776, *An Enquiry into the Nature and Causes of the Wealth of Nations*, http://www.gutenberg.org/files/3300/3300-h/3300-h.htm.

Soja, Edward, 2010, *Seeking Spatial Justice*, Minneapolis: University of Minnesota Press.

Somerville, P., and Steele, A., 2002, *'Race', Housing & Social Exclusion*, London: Jessica Kingsley Publishers.

Spartacus Network of Disability Researchers and Campaigners, 2012, *The People's Review of the Work Capability Assessment*, www.ekklesia.co.uk/node/19621.

Stevenson, Kenneth, 2000, *Abba Father: Understanding and Using the Lord's Prayer*, Norwich: Canterbury Press.

Stratford, Tim (ed.), 2006, *Worship, Window of the Urban Church*, London: SPCK.

Taylor, Patton, 2004, 'The 174 Story', in Eastman, Michael, and Latham, Steve (eds), *Urban Church: A Practitioner's Resource Book*, London: SPCK.

Tertullian, 'De Oratione I', in Roberts, A., and Donaldson, J. (eds), 1993, *The Ante-Nicene Fathers, Vol. III*, Edinburgh: T&T Clark.

Thompson, Anna, 2012, 'Holy Sofas: Transformational Encounters between Evangelical Christians and Post-Christendom Urban Communities', *Practical Theology*, 5.1, pp. 47–70.

Townsend, P., 1979, *Poverty in the United Kingdom*, London: Penguin Books.

Tunstall, Rebecca, and Coulter, Alice, 2006, *Twenty-five Years on Twenty Estates – Turning the Tide?*, LSE and Joseph Rowntree Foundation, Cambridge: The Polity Press.

Upton, Julie, 2014, Report in *NetLink*, NECN's Summer 2014 newsletter, www.nationalestatechurches.org.

van Kempen, Ronald, *et al.* (eds), 2005, *Restructuring Large Housing Estates in Europe*, Bristol: The Policy Press.

Vincent, John J., 2004, *Radical Jesus: The Way of Jesus – Then and Now*, Sheffield: Ashram Press.

Vincent, John J. (ed.), 2003, *Faithfulness in the City*, Haywarden: Monad Press.

Winter, Jane, 2014, 'Why Does the Church Appear to Ignore the Potential for Indigenous Ministry in Areas of Social Housing?', unpublished paper.

Wood, Martin, 2008, 'Strategic Planning or Piecemeal Development? A Study of the Establishment of Church of England Parishes and Their Churches in the New Town of Basildon between 1949 and 1964', MA Thesis, University of Wales, Lampeter.

Woolf, Virginia, 1938, *Three Guineas*, Eugene: Harvest House Books (reprint 1963).

A selection of websites relating to our subject

Catholic Social Action Together (CSAN): www.csan.org.uk
Christian Coalition for Urban Mission: www.urbanmission.org.uk
Christians Against Poverty: www.capuk.org
Church Action on Poverty: www.church-poverty.org.uk
Church Urban Fund: www.cuf.org.uk
Crucible Courses: www.cruciblecourse.org.uk
CURBS: www.curbsproject.org.uk
Eden Network: www.eden-network.org
Friends of the Poor in South India: www.fpsindia.btck.co.uk
Frontier Youth Trust: www.fyt.org.uk
Housing Justice: www.housingjustice.org.uk
InnerCHANGE: www.innerchange.org
Laurie Green: www.lauriegreen.org
Legacy Youth Congregation: www.legacyweb.org
Livability: www.communitymission.org.uk
Living Wage: www.livingwage.org.uk
National Estate Churches Network (NECN): www.nationalestatechurches.org
Quaker Social Action: www.quakersocialaction.com
UNLOCK: www.unlock-urban.org.uk
Urban Expression: www.urbanexpression.org.uk
Urban Presence: www.urbanpresence.org.uk
Urban Theology Unit: www.utusheffield.org.uk
West Malling, St Mary's Benedictine Abbey: www.mallingabbey.org

Biblical References Index

Subject Index